OXFORD MEDICAL PUBLICATIONS

Back Pain

THE FACTS

Third edition

D0293788

Back Pain

THE FACTS
Third Edition

MALCOLM I.V. JAYSON
Rheumatic Diseases Centre
University of Manchester

Line drawings
by
Richard Neave

OXFORD NEW YORK TOKYO
OXFORD UNIVERSITY PRESS

Oxford University Press, Walton Street, Oxford OX2 6DP

Oxford New York Toronto
Delhi Bombay Calcutta Madras Karachi
Petaling Jaya Singapore Hong Kong Tokyo
Nairobi Dar es Salaam Cape Town
Melbourne Auckland

and associated companies in
Berlin Ibadan

Oxford is a trade mark of Oxford University Press

Published in the United States
by Oxford University Press, New York
First published 1981
Second edition 1987
© Malcolm I. V. Jayson, 1981, 1987, 1992
Third edition 1992
Reprinted 1993

A catalogue record for this book is available from the British Library

Library of Congress Cataloging in Publication Data
Jayson, Malcolm I. V.
Back pain: the facts / Malcolm I. V. Jayson; line drawings by
Richard Neave.—3rd ed.
(Oxford medical publications)
Includes index.
(pbk.)
1. Backache—Popular works. I. Title. II. Series.
RD771.B217J39   1992   617.5'64—dc20   92–14481
ISBN 0-19-262249-8
ISBN 0-19-262248-X (pbk.)

Printed in Great Britain by
Biddles Ltd, Guildford and King's Lynn

To Judi, Dinah, Gordon, Robs, Jessica, and Joseph.

Foreword to the second edition

by
CHARLES PHELPS
Imperial College, University of London

Some time ago, I 'slipped a disc'. I could not point to any immediate incident as a cause; I woke one morning with some discomfort in one leg and when I got up I found that I could not move freely. I felt particularly aggrieved because this was at a time when I was hoping to tidy my mother's house prior to sale and to build a wall in the garden of my own house. I soon found these had to be abandoned. After a little wifely nagging, I went to the doctor who examined me and gave the curiously euphemistic diagnosis: I had a 'slipped' disc.

I tell this not because I wish to excite sympathy, but to produce my credentials for joining the club of 'back pain sufferers'. Quite apart from the restrictive physical practices to which I had to become accustomed, there were other perplexities. Why the smile when I hobbled into a room? There was a faint but unmistakable suggestion that I was a species of malingerer and that my problems could not possibly be as incommoding as I made out.

It was the first time I had been stricken with anything that changed the quality of my life. Now there were things I could and could not do physically. The advice I was given made it clear this was not something that would get better in the time-scale of recovery from flu: about a year, if I took care of myself, I was told.

The other feature I noted was that unless I wanted to shackle myself in hospital, self-help was the order of the day. Where did this start? For me, in trying to understand what had gone wrong. Perhaps man travelled through the evolutionary time-scale too rapidly from his happily buoyant position in water through the stability of a four-legged design on dry land to this two-legged defiance of gravity, and therefore we all have a cryptic tendency to structural failure. Whatever the story, I would recommend this excellent book by Professor Jayson for all who wonder at the disabling nature of these human structural disorders. A knowledge of the cause of the problem predisposes the sufferer to adopt postures (both physical and mental) that can intelligently aid the process of recovery.

It is fashionable to believe that most diseases have an explanation ultimately revealing a fault at the molecular level. There is ample evidence for such a belief when we come to study, for instance, some hereditary diseases and a number of bacterial ailments. It is altogether more difficult to travel along a reductionist pathway in explaining the failure of structural systems, and the reason for this is implicit in the word *systems*. Just as it would be difficult to produce, *intact*, the individual elements from a prestressed concrete girder, so it is not yet possible (and may never be) to reconstruct the working physiological system from the assortment of specific molecules of which it is composed.

Research has produced an abundant understanding of what goes to make up the connective tissues of the body. The molecular components have been minutely described and the geography of their occurrence in tissues such as intervertebral discs of cartilage is well understood. A start has been made in modelling connective tissue, in an attempt to understand how the particular blend of components can in one mixture make bone, whilst in another cartilage or intervertebral disc. The analogy with the prestressed girder can be pursued: the dry cement and sand and steel reinforcements correspond to the molecular components of a tissue. When water is mixed and certain spatial arrangements are made, a girder can become capable of supporting structures, which neither concrete nor steel alone would do. It is when we come to do this reconstruction process with our biological systems that we cannot yet claim success, and one of the most exciting areas of research is finding out why we cannot reproduce the properties of the whole from the sum of the parts.

I spent a good part of my scientific life attempting to solve problems such as I have just posed. I and the countless number of other research workers here and abroad recognize the importance of fundamental enquiry and thereby the need for money in supporting the experiments which must be set up. In the case of back pain, charitable trusts in the United Kingdom deserve special mention and bodies such as the Arthritis and Rheumatism Council, and the Nuffield and Wellcome Trusts all have generously supported what may often have looked like inauspicious ventures. Just as the molecules that make up the system are diverse, so are the talents of the research investigators. It is a marvellous human meeting-ground of, among others, engineers, surgeons, physicians, immunologists, anatomists, biophysicists, and biochemists, from whose committed perseverance to the problem of skeletal disorders come spin-offs additional to those of pure science. Because of such multidisciplinary research, the secretary sits a little more comfortably in her chair, the orthopaedic aids are a little better designed, and new materials for hip replacements appear.

But progress in research is gradual, as is recovery from these disabilities, so we should not expect overnight miracles. However, the optimism that all good scientists have must surely see to it that the presently intractable problems of back pain are eventually solved.

Preface to the third edition

Back pain is so common and widespread that it is no exaggeration to say that nearly everybody suffers from it sooner or later. It is very difficult to comprehend the immensity of the problem, as back pain occurs at all ages and in all levels of society. More days off work are lost because of back troubles than for almost any other reason and this is so not only for the manual labourer but also for those with relatively 'soft' jobs, such as office executives.

Pain in the back is not a new phenomenon. Studies of skeletons from archaeological remains show precisely the same types of change that occur today. The writings of the ancient Greek physicians describe very similar problems and indeed some of their forms of treatment are not so very different from those that we still use. Even examination of the skeletons of animals such as the enormous dinosaur in the Natural History Museum in London reveal similar types of wear and tear in the spine.

Although the back problem has been known for such a long time it is only quite recently that its importance has emerged and we have begun to appreciate the amount of suffering and the economic burden it produces. Increasingly the medical profession is asked how to prevent the development of back pain, how to pick out those who are likely to suffer from it, and the best forms of treatment. As soon as we start to ask these questions we realize that not all back pains are the same and that this symptom can develop for many different reasons. Some of these are clear cut and obvious but in many instances we are unable to sort out the precise cause of the trouble in the individual sufferer.

Modern science is increasingly aware of the need for further research in this field and the subject is of interest not only to physicians and surgeons but also pathologists, radiologists, psychologists, biochemists, bioengineers, and many other disciplines. In the long run, the only way to achieve real advances is a proper understanding of what causes the pain and why it has happened. Often opinions are expressed, particularly by non-medical practitioners, that are not based upon scientific fact but rather on personal concepts which have not been tested in an acceptable way. Many of the myths that surround the whole subject arise because such views are put forward didactically and without the critical self-examination that is normally expected in medical circles. This lax approach applies equally to the many forms of treatment used for back pain sufferers. No acknowledgement is made of the fact that most episodes of back pain improve or get completely better spontaneously. It is a bit like having a cold and taking medicine X: even though X is completely valueless, one can be sure that the cold will get better within a week or so. Many claims are made for the efficacy of various types of treatment without appreciating the natural improvements and fluctuations in the pain that normally occur. Individual anecdotal stories of dramatic improvements after different types of treatment abound, yet studies to demonstrate their true effectiveness can tell a very different story. The persistence of the back problem, despite all the claims made, points to the considerable difficulties with which we are faced. I firmly believe in the identification of the cause of the back pain in the individual and prescribing and determining the values of the appropriate forms of treatment for that particular problem. Modern ideas about pain and its control help us to understand and develop various types of treatment to control pain irrespective of the cause. Although this approach is very helpful in relieving symptoms it cannot solve the problem, as the basic causes are not tackled.

Advice for the back sufferer is plentiful. This book has been written to give the reader deeper insight into the whole problem. It endeavours to explain current views on the causes of back pain and the significance of the various changes that occur in the spine. I have described the various types of treatment that are in common use and reviewed whether they really work. It does seem possible to minimize the back problem with postural and ergonomic advice and this also is included.

In the last few years our understanding of back problems has advanced dramatically. In part this is due to modern technology – the new CAT scans and Magnetic Resonance Image scans, and new types of biochemical and pathological investigations. However, perhaps the greatest change is one of the attitudes of medical and scientific workers towards the problem. There is now real interest in understanding what causes back pain and in evaluating new and traditional types of treatment. This third edition describes all the latest advances. The new imaging methods are illustrated together with the techniques for full diagnosis and assessment. There are new forms of minimal invasive surgery. The most dramatic changes are for patients with chronic persistent back pain. This new edition describes our latest knowledge explaining why some people suffer persistent problems, and presents in detail the new approaches towards rehabilitation and the success that may be achieved.

Back pain is the commonest form of rheumatism and its control is the biggest challenge in rheumatology. A proper understanding of what is happening is crucial for further medical advances. I hope that this book will be of help to back sufferers and stimulate further interest in the topic.

Rheumatic Diseases Centre   M.I.V.J.
University of Manchester
June 1992

Contents

Plates

1

Structure and function of the human spine

During evolution the animal kingdom split into two main groups: the invertebrates and the vertebrates. The invertebrates possess no internal skeleton but instead have a tough outer shell or exoskeleton. The various parts of the limbs and trunk articulate with one another and movement is provided by muscles attached on the inside of this outer case. Such a structure is found in countless species, including insects and shellfish. In some the exoskeleton has become thick and tough, providing protection for the internal tissues and acting as a suit of armour. However, the rigidity of this system produces considerable problems. For example a rigid system such as this cannot accommodate growth. A change of skeleton must take place at regular intervals. The very nature of the joints between rigid segments allows the animal to produce stereotyped movements but severely restricts its ability to adapt and evolve in relation to altered environmental conditions. These constraints have left the invertebrates relatively lowly members of the animal kingdom.

In contrast the vertebrates have an internal skeleton. In the trunk there is a backbone or vertebral column and in the limbs the various long bones. This skeleton grows with the animal and is flexible, as its components are connected by various types of joints designed according to the requirements at each site. Muscles, ligaments, and other structures are attached to this internal skeleton and can produce a subtlety and complexity of movements that are lacking in invertebrates. This type of structure can be seen in primitive animals such as the lancet, coelacanth, and even the modern dogfish. Natural selection has allowed the more successful species to flourish at the expense of those less well adapted to their environment. This process of evolution has led to the development of modern species of fish, amphibians, reptiles, birds, and mammals. The internal skeletons of all these diverse groups show similar fundamental structures but with extreme adaptations to the species' way of life.

Nearly all animals walk on four limbs with the trunk horizontal. Man is almost unique in standing upright balanced on two limbs. The advantages of this posture are obvious but clearly it also leads to considerable stresses on the skeleton. This alone could be responsible for many of the back problems that we suffer today. That is not to say that animals do not suffer from backache. Communication is difficult but we do know that dachshunds with their long and relatively poorly supported spines are very prone to this problem.

If the upright posture was responsible for producing spinal problems you would not expect natural selection to have favoured the vertical position and we would all be walking on four limbs. However, the span of life during most of the period of man's evolution was only some 20 to 30 years. As the majority of back problems occur at an older age, back pain would hardly affect the evolutionary process.

The functions of the human spine

The backbone or vertebral column is the principal supporting structure in the human body. Both upper and lower limbs are attached to it through a complex series of joints. The ribs are attached to the spine in the back of the chest wall in such a way that contraction of muscles allows co-ordinated expansion of the chest and breathing. Muscles, ligaments, and tendons connect various parts of the spine to each other and other structures, allowing a wide variety of movements.

In order to see the structure of the vertebral column, one can do no better than look at the work of Andreas Vesalius. He was an anatomist born in Brussels and was a professor in Louvain and Padua. He produced a magnificent book in 1543 entitled *De Humani Corporis Fabrica*—the Structure of the Human body. This was a new departure in the study of anatomy, as it was based entirely on dissection. This volume is remarkable for its illustrations by Italian draughtsmen. There is a large series of plates that illustrate human anatomy in superb detail. One of the joys of these drawings is the sense of emotion in the postures of the subjects (Fig.1) Many of the plates include a background against which the subject is posed and the separate plates can be joined together to give a panoramic view of Tuscany in the sixteenth century.

The spine has to carry a heavy load. At any level it is the vertebral column which is principally responsible for transmitting the weight of the body above and any loads being lifted or carried. When muscles contract to produce movements or stabilize joints, there is often additional stress on the vertebral column. The spine is, however, remarkably flexible. It can bend forwards, backwards, and sideways and it can twist. Often these movements are undertaken in complex combinations and with load-bearing at the same time.

The spinal cord emerges from the base of the brain and passes downwards through the vertebral column. It subdivides into nerve roots which emerge through spaces between the vertebrae (Fig. 2). These nerves will reach virtually every body tissue. They carry information from the tissues to the spinal cord and then to the brain, allowing perception of sensations. In turn messages from the brain are carried back down the spinal cord and along the nerves to activate muscles and produce movements. The spinal cord is an extremely delicate and complicated structure. It is protected against damage by lying within a column of bony arches in the back of the spine. This is known as the vertebral canal. The nerve roots separate from the spinal cord and pass obliquely downwards to emerge from the vertebral canal through openings know as invertebral foramina. Despite the complex movements undertaken by the spine, normally no damage to the spinal cord or nerve roots will arise.

Apart from the structural functions of the vertebral column is the requirement that it should function for a lifetime of perhaps 70 or 80 years or even more. With all the wonders of modern science are there any man-made materials that could stand up to such use for that period of time? Can modern designers and engineers produce comparable structures that would still work after all those years? Our cars have problems after two or three years and their average life is only about eight to ten years.

There is an extremely important difference between the living skeleton and mechanical structures such as motor car engines. In an engine, wear and tear changes occur with use but the worn parts have no ability to repair themselves. The moving components work less effectively and eventually may break down. Their function can only be restored by some form of mechanical correction such as putting in a new part. In contrast, the living components of the human spine are constantly being renewed. Normally this happens very slowly but over the years the skeleton, as with all body tissues, is

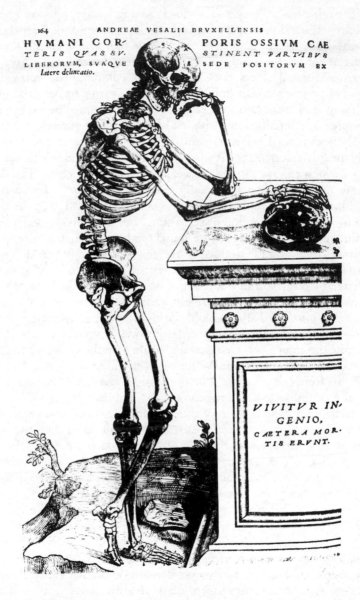

Fig. 1 The human skeleton. Illustration from *De Humani Corporis Fabrica* by Andreas Vesalius (1543)

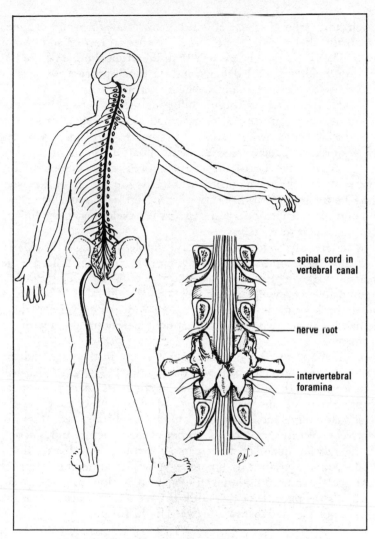

spinal cord in
vertebral canal

nerve root

intervertebral
foramina

Fig. 2 The vertebral column, spinal cord, and nerve roots

completely replaced. When there is an injury this process acceler-
ates—in other words the damaged tissues are rapidly repaired. An
obvious example is to compare a break of a piston rod in an engine
and a fracture of a human bone. The only way to repair the engine is
to dismantle it and change the piston rod for a new one. However,
in the human skeleton, around the broken bone ends the tissues

which form the bone swell and grow and form new bone. Eventually the two bone ends fuse together to form a solid bone again. The repair can be stronger than the original bone before the fracture. Evidence of the damage and the repair process can be seen on X-rays for many years and is usually permanent.

Various types of repair occur following wear and tear changes in the spine. It is unfortunate that sometimes the repair process is excessive and leads to alterations in structure and function of the spine. For many patients pain is caused in part by the original injury but is principally due to the repair processes. Examples of this happening and producing problems include the growth of excessive bony tissue around worn joints pressing on nerves and ligaments and chronic inflammation and scar tissue developing in the linings covering the nerve roots.

In children the spine is flexible and supple whereas in the elderly it usually has become stiff and much more unyielding. What are the changes that take place and why do they occur? Do they inevitably accompany growing older? Are these changes the cause of back pain and is back pain inevitable? Are there ways of preventing these changes or are current forms of treatment merely tinkering with the problems?

In this book the things that can go wrong in the back and the ways they may produce pain will be described. There is much still to be learned as the study of back pain is still in its infancy. A lot has been written about the changes that occur but often these are personal opinions and have not or cannot be substantiated. It is only relatively recently that detailed studies of the structure and function of the human spine, of what can go wrong, how back pain is produced, and testing of the true values of different forms of treatment have been undertaken. Progress is slow but real for all that. It is the purpose of this book to give a factual account of the current position and the ways forward in the future.

The vertebral column

We all think of man as being upright and indeed sometimes apply moral values to this posture! However, simple observation will show that the spine is not straight but has a number of curves. The low back or lumbar region is slightly hollowed so that it is curved backwards. This is known technically as the lumbar lordosis. The back of the chest is curved slightly forward and the neck points slightly forwards. In the various problems that arise in the spine this normal pattern may change. The curves may be lost or exaggerated. There may be an abnormal curvature forwards—a kyphosis, a sideways twist—a scoliosis, or there may be a sharp kink. Not only do these abnormal postures develop due to various types of disease, but also they may make things worse by altering the ways in which the spine works and placing stresses on parts of the spine not designed to deal with them.

The spine consists of a column óf bony blocks known as vertebrae standing one on top of the other (Fig. 3). In the neck there are seven which are known as cervical vertebrae; there are twelve in the back of the chest—the dorsal or thoracic vertebrae; and five in the back—the lumbar vertebrae. The bottom or fifth lumbar vertebra (L5) is directly attached to the sacrum or tail bone. The sacrum is the back part of the pelvis, a ring of bone providing support for the spine and trunk.

All the vertebrae have similar basic structures but with considerable variations at each level, reflecting the different functions at each site. For example, the neck is remarkably flexible and only has to bear the weight of the skull. The cervical vertebrae are very lightly built and shaped so as to allow a considerable range of movement between them. In contrast the back has to bear the weight of the trunk and transmits forceful movements of the body. The lumbar vertebrae are much thicker and tougher structures with relatively limited movements allowed between them (Fig. 4).

Each vertebra consists of a cylindrical part in front known as the vertebral body. This has flat upper and lower surfaces known as the vertebral end-plates. The vertebral body is convex in the front and flattened behind. This flattened area forms the front part of the canal down which the spinal cord and nerve roots pass. The vertebral arch surrounds the rest of the canal giving protection to the structures within. Each vertebra is joined to those above and below by joints between the vertebral bodies and between the arches.

The intervertebral disc lies between the vertebral end-plates. It is a cushion of tissue that normally provides a springy and movable connection between the bones. Three types of movement occur at this cushion—flattening under loads, bending, and twisting. However, unlike a cushion the disc has a very definite structure that is all-important when things go wrong. Basically the disc consists of two parts: a central area known as the nucleus pulposus and an outer ring, the annulus fibrosus.

In his drawings of the spine Vesalius showed the structure of the disc and realized that it was complex (Fig. 5). He knew that the

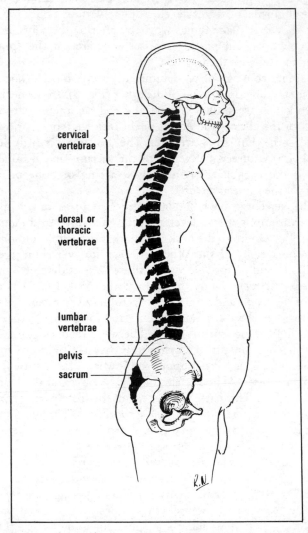

Fig. 3 The vertebrae of the spine

outermost layer is different from the inner material but he did not get the details absolutely right. The nucleus consists of jelly-like material containing a few tangled fibres and many large molecules

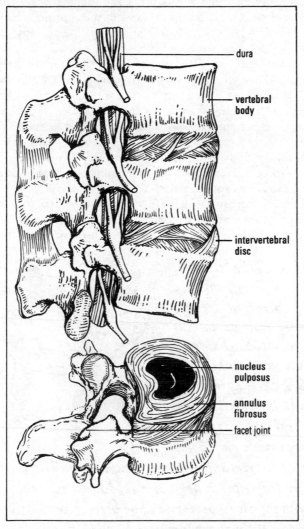

Fig. 4 The vertebrae joined by the invertebral discs and the pairs of facet joints. The nerve roots run down the vertebral canal within the dura and emerge from the spine through the invertebral foramina.

known as proteoglycans. The nucleus has the property of all gelatinous materials, namely that it can be squashed and then alters in shape but its total volume will reman constant. The nucleus is kept in shape by the outer annular ring and the vertebral end-plates above and below. This allows it to transmit the enormous loads that may be carried by the spine. It is the nature of the proteoglycans in the nucleus that they are constantly trying to suck in water and swell. This tendency is resisted by pressures produced by the weight of the body. When we sleep lying horizontally at night this swelling process is unimpeded. It is a fact that we are slightly taller when we first rise in the morning than at the end of the day. This process is carried to the extreme in astronants who after several days of weightlessness may grow by a couple of inches. As their space suits are individually and very precisely designed this produced considerable difficulties and a lot of complaints from the astronants before the cause was appreciated.

The annulus fibrosus which surrounds the nucleus has quite a different structure. It consists mainly of fibres of collagen. This is a fibrous protein which is uniquely designed for tensile or stretching

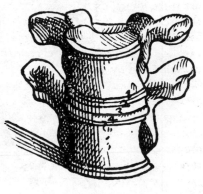

Vt leuiori negocio, quæ bic pertracto, affequaris, duas è thorace uertebras, anteriori facie ex puerili corpore depictas habes. In quibus 1 notat fuperioris uertebræ cartilaginem, fui corporis inferiorē appen dicem, ipfumǵ corpus in, teruenientem, 2 eiufdē uer tebræ humiliorem appendicem, 3 cartilagineū ligamentum, fuperioris inferiorisǵ uertebræ appēdices intercedēs, 4 fu periorem inferioris uertebræ appēdicem, 5 cartilaginem, di ctam modo appendicem fuæ uertebræ copulantem.

Fig. 5 The structure of the intervertebral disc as drawn by Vesalius in 1543

strength. A collagen fibre is considerably stronger than a steel wire of the same dimensions. The collagen fibres of the annulus are attached around the edge of the vertebral end-plate and spiral obliquely upwards and downwards to the end-plates above and below. They cross over and interweave one another in a complex fashion so forming an extremely strong network that surrounds the nucleus. When vertical loads are placed on the spine the nucleus is squashed and slightly flattened and the annular ring will expand slightly, but nevertheless will not give way. Indeed, the annulus is so strong that under extreme load it is the vertebral end-plates that will fracture rather than the annulus itself. This criss-cross arrangement of annular fibres allows relatively easily the movements of bending forwards and backwards and to the side. However, twisting movements are more difficult. This is one of the reasons why back problems are more likely to arise with this type of activity.

At the back of the spine the vertebral arches are also joined to the arches above and below by the small facet joints. There is one joint on each side at each level so that connecting each pair of vertebrae are three joints: one between the vertebral bodies and two between the arches. The facet joints differ from the intervertebral disc in that they are synovial joints. The opposing joint surfaces are covered by cartilage or gristle and are connected to each other by a fibrous capsule lined by a layer of tissue known as the synovial membrane. Within the joint is a lubricant known as the synovial fluid which allows the joint surfaces to move against each other. This arrangement is very similar to that of the joints in the limbs, although the sizes and shapes of the various joints differ enormously. Any movement between a pair of vertebrae must involve all three joints; it is not possible for one of these joints to move to the exclusion of the others. It may seem trite to point this out but one often hears statements that one of these joints alone is stiff or that manipulation is applied to a single joint, ignoring the movements that must take place at the others.

The vertebrae are also joined to one another by a series of ligaments which ensheath the bodies and connect the arches. These ligaments are relatively flexible and yet have an important role in covering the bony and joint surfaces.

A pile of vertebrae one on top of the other is intrinsically unstable and one can readily imagine how bowing or slipping of the structure

could occur. The spine is stabilized by very powerful muscles
attached to the vertebrae, the pelvis, and the back of the chest wall.
An interesting analogy is with the stays on a yacht which have a
remarkably similar function in stiffening and stabilizing the mast
(Fig. 6). During any exertion these muscles contract so stiffening the
spine and enabling it to bear the load.

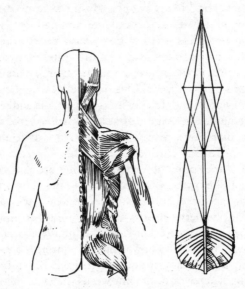

Fig. 6 The stabilization of the spine by muscles is remarkably similar to the
stiffening of the mast of a yacht by the stays

The spinal cord emerges from the base of the brain and passes
down through the vertebral canal behind the vertebral bodies and
is surrounded by the vertebral arches (Fig. 2). During the passage
downwards nerve roots separate off to emerge through the
intervertebral foramina between the vertebral arches at every level.
The spinal cord itself finally ends at about the junction between the
first and second lumbar vertebrae (L1/2) and below that level there
are only nerve roots in the vertebral canal. The roots emerge from
the canal and pass on to their ultimate destinations, uniting and
dividing in complex fashions to form the nerves which supply all the
structures of the human body.

The spinal cord and nerve roots are not in direct contact with the
bony vertebral canal but are covered by several protective sheaths.

The outermost is known as the dura mater and is a strong fibrous membrane which forms a wide tubular sheath around the spinal cord and the upper part of the nerve roots with tubular prolongations along the nerve roots themselves as they pass out through the intervertebral foramina. Inside the dura is the arachnoid which is a much more delicate membrane loosely investing the spinal cord and nerve roots. The innermost layer is known as the pia and is intimately adherent to the spinal cord and nerve roots. In the course of various back disorders these coverings may become inflamed and thickened with a lot of scar tissue. This is known as arachnoiditis and can be the cause of severe pain in the back and in the areas in the legs that the nerves supply.

The spine itself also has a nerve supply. Tiny branches from the nerve roots will supply the ligaments around the spine, the capsule or surroundings of the facet joints, the dura, arachnoid, and pia coats around the spinal cord and the blood vessels in the bone marrow. Surprisingly they do not occur in the substance of the intervertebral disc but only in the outer layers of the annulus fibrosus. As damage to a nerve fibre is a prerequisite to produce the sensation of pain, it is clear that most disorders of the disc alone will be painless. The presence of damage to a disc seen on X-rays does not mean that this has been the cause of back pain. It is only when a disc disorder produces damage spreading to the disc edge or to the surrounding structures that pain may develop.

Another point about the nerve supply to the spine is that the nerves from each level combine with one another in extremely complex fashions. This produces the phenomenon known as cross-innervation which means that any nerve may carry information about abnormalities arising at several different levels. For this reason it is often extremely difficult to localize the source of symptons felt in the back. Pain felt at one site can be due to a problem in a quite different area. Considerable circumspection is required when trying to identify the source of pain in the back pain sufferer.

The stresses on the spine

Because of the obvious practical problems it is remarkably difficult to gain objective information about exactly how the spine transmits load. Most of the data is derived from experiments conducted in Sweden on volunteers in whom fine needles were inserted into the intervertebral discs. The pressures developed during a variety of physical activites were recorded. As would be expected the lowest levels of pressure in the nucleus were found when lying down. High pressures developed when standing upright and even higher when carrying a heavy load. There were very high levels when sitting upright: the highest recorded were when sitting, bending forwards, and carrying a heavy load. In some people the total load on the disc was about 340 kg or about a third of a ton. The pressures developed could be related directly to posture, the load carried, and the contraction of the muscles stabilizing the spine. The posture of the back seems all-important. We know that a properly designed back-rest will relieve a lot of strain in the spine and in these experiments they found that a properly designed back-rest or a good chair with a proper spinal suport could significantly reduce the pressure within the disc during sitting. This knowledge is used by designers to improve the comfort of car seats and other chairs.

Another way of getting at the problem is by measuring the pressures within the tummy or abdomen. At rest, the pressure in the abdomen is low. During exercise we forcibly contract the abdominal muscles and hold our breath, so contracting the diaphragm and increasing the pressure within the abdomen. Why do we do this? By increasing the pressure we convert the abdominal cavity into a high-pressure ball capable of carrying some of the body load. A pressurized ball, such as a blown-up rugby football, will bear load and one could even sit on it without squashing it—that is, it will carry the weight of the body. On the other hand, if it is not blown up or has a leak and is under low pressure, by sitting on it one would flop on the ground—in other words low-pressure balls carry weight poorly. In a similar way, increasing the pressure in the abdomen allows a proportion of the body load to be transmitted through the abdomen and so relieves the spine to a certain extent. Weight-lifters put on tightly a strong leather cummerbund just prior to their lift. They do this in order to raise the pressure within the abdomen so that part of the weight is carried through the abdomen thus reducing somewhat the load on the spine. Part of the benefit from wearing lumbar corsets is due to their tightness increasing the abdominal pressure, again protecting the back in the same way.

The increase of the pressure within the abdomen is proportional to the total load on the trunk. This concept has been used to measure the stresses associated with various activities. Initially, measurements of the pressure within the abdomen were made using a balloon and a fine tube inserted through the anus and connected to an outside measuring instrument. Today there are sophisticated electronic measuring instruments that look like small pills and can be swallowed. Not only does the radio-pill measure the pressures but also it contains a tiny radio-transmitter and the signals can be picked up by a special radio receiver. The pills are safe and are eventually passed in the motions.

Most mechanical studies of the spine have been performed using post-mortem material. Clearly this information must be interpreted with caution as the dead spine is very different from that in life. In fact such studies have helped enormously in identifying the areas of potential weakness and where the stresses are most concentrated. They have shown that the back of the spine and particularly the arches carry a disproportionately large amount of the total body load and that this is increased by bending backwards. A careful examination of the spine will often reveal the evidence of damage produced by this means. This may take the form of small fractures of the bone or damage to the facet joints (Fig. 4).

The pressures that have been recorded within the disc are not normally sufficient to damage the outer annulus fibrosus and cause bursting or prolapse. Indeed, they are much more likely to damage the vertebral end-plates, than the disc itself. Nevertheless, it is possible the repetitive loads could cause fatigue failure of the fibres of the annulus fibrosus. This phenomenon known as fatigue failure affects many materials when stressed. Engineers have become well aware of it. If a piece of metal wire is bent and straightened once, its strength remains intact. However, if this bending and straightening is repeated many times the metal becomes fatigued and eventually may give way very easily. The same changes may occur in the intervertebral disc. We know that stresses on the disc are concentrated much more at the back than at the front and fatigue failure of the fibres may occur in this area. It therefore seems that repetitive loads can lead to weakening of the disc so that eventually some stress makes it finally give way.

In such a complex system with innumerable components, each serving important roles and interrelating with one another, it is hardly surprising that problems may arise. These may be due to abnormalities of development, damage due to excess forces, wear and tear damage due to repetitive use, and other problems. Subsequent chapters will deal with these various aspects and indicate the current limits of our understanding about them.

The causes of back pain

Failure to appreciate that every back pain is different and that there are many reasons why back pain occurs leads to much confusion. A form of treatment suitable for one problem may be useless for another so we must try to determine the underlying cause. Back pain is a symptom just as being short of breath is a symptom. In thinking about how to treat breathlessness we would need to know whether the patient had bronchitis, asthma, tuberculosis, lung cancer, heart disease, or other problems. In the same way we should always try to establish the cause of the back pain, although admittedly this can be extremely difficult.

Pain may be felt in the back due to disease in the back itself or it may be a result of some internal abnormality but felt in the back. Gynaecological disorders may sometimes produce quite severe back symptoms and these are usually worse at the time of the menstrual periods.

There are a number of different broad groups of disorders of the spine that may lead to back pain. They include mechanical and structural problems as already mentioned; inflammation, which can be the result of infection, or other inflammatory disorders such as ankylosing spondylitis or rheumatoid arthritis; disorders of the structure of the bones of the spine; and tumours of various sorts that may occur in and around the back. Each of these groups includes a number of different disorders which will be described in this book.

The big problem is that there are many back sufferers in whom it is not possible to identify the cause of the symptoms. If such patients are seen by different physicians and surgeons, physiotherapists, osteopaths, and chiropractors, they may be given various diagnoses and the terms used are often quite different. A wide variety of different types of treatment may be offered. The patient may be perplexed and become more confused with every specialist he sees. The truth of the matter is that for many back problems, and particularly those that are relatively minor, it is not possible to identify the source of the problem. Although words such as fibrositis, adhesions, sacro-iliac strain, lumbo-sacral strain, etc. imply knowledge of what is actually wrong they have no scientific foundation and the various types of disorders have not been proven on examination of the spine by pathologists. My personal view is that with this degree of uncertainty it is better to be honest with the patient and oneself and label the problem as 'non-specific back pain'. With newer diagnostic methods we are identifying with accuracy various problems within this group so that the number of patients in whom this uncertainty exists is slowly shrinking.

2

Back pain in society

The severity of backache ranges from minor niggles to excrutiating pain but the problem as a whole is remarkably widespread. Accurate figures seem impossible but recent surveys in Britain, Europe, and North America showed that the symptom is experienced at some stage in life by between 80 and almost 100 per cent of the entire population. Any discussion on the subject almost inevitably brings out personal stories of individual suffering. In one survey conducted recently 21 per cent or over a fifth of the subjects questioned had suffered from back symptoms within the previous fortnight. Although many had relatively minor problems this must mean that most of us must suffer from back pain sooner or later. The back problem alone significantly interferes with enjoyment of life and with work in a large proportion of the population.

It is not enough simply to be aware that backache is common. We need to know the severity and extent of the problem and its relation to different types of work. This information is required not only for developing treatment services, but also to provide guidance with regard to occupational hazards and postural problems, on the premise that prevention is better than treatment. At first sight it would seem relatively easy to determine the severity of the back pain problem. However, there is a large number of complicating factors making such studies difficult and leading to a variety of ways of interpreting the results. It is worth explaining certain of these difficulties in some detail so that the conclusions drawn from such studies will be seen in a more realistic perspective.

Drawbacks of back pain surveys

Pain is an unpleasant emotional state felt in the mind but identified as arising in a part of the body. In other words it is a subjective sensation. The pain from, say, a boil occurs in the brain. Without the mind the pain would not exist, only an area of swelling and inflammation. Pain is a defence mechanism designed to make the sufferer protect an injured part from further damage. Sometimes, however, the mind can make a mistake and feels pain when no cause exists or fails to feel pain when there is good reason. There are reasons for this which will be explained in Chapter 6. Because messages reach the brain by a very complicated network of nerves which connect with one another in various ways, the mind may place the sensation as arising in the wrong place.

In other words back pain is a subjective sensation felt and described by the sufferer and there is no objective means by which the pain can be proven. The doctor must either believe or disbelieve the patient's statement, whether or not there are obvious things wrong with the back. In contrast a survey of, say, tuberculosis of the lung can rely on hard evidence of the disease shown by a chest X-ray.

To prove the presence of back pain it is not enough to show that the back does not move properly or that an X-ray is abnormal. One person may have a completely rigid spine which is pain-free and another a back that is remarkably flexible and yet he is severely troubled by back pain. The relationship between symptoms of back pain and wear and tear changes on X-ray is extremely poor.

This means that the only real test for back pain is whether the subject can reliably describe it. Most people do not tell lies when questioned on a topic such as this. However, we all feel things differently and interpret pain sensations in different ways. There is enormous variation in the ways we respond to particular stimuli and this must mean that the reporting of pain sensations will differ greatly from person to person.

Different people feel pain to different extents. Some of us, with a so-called high pain threshold, can tolerate a stimulus such as pressure or a needle prick that another with a low pain threshold may find extremely painful. These differences between all of us depend upon a number of factors. They may be partly racial or cultural, reflecting the normal and acceptable forms of behaviour in our society. The ways in which we feel pain may reflect other problems and anxieties which may not be very apparent. I know that if I am about to go on holiday I will ignore a bit of backache whereas if I am facing a difficult or unpleasant day it may seem very much worse.

As pain is a sensation which cannot be proven it is sometimes used as an excuse to avoid work or provide a day off. We have all heard of how the incidence of back pain seems to increase when there is an important football match or race meeting. Undoubtedly this sometimes happens but it is impossible to know how often back pain is falsely used in this way. Individual cases when they are known, tend to stand out, but my feeling is that the risk as a whole is somewhat overstated.

Many surveys of back pain will ask if the individual has ever suffered from this problem. There is a natural process in the mind to obliterate memories of painful events. The most extreme examples of this occur with severe accidents leading to unconsciousness. After recovery there may be complete loss of memory for the accident and for the events leading up to it. We often find that people will forget attacks of back pain in a similar way but to a much lesser extent. Poor recall of information about previous attacks of back pain can lead to serious underestimates of the frequency of this problem. As back pain usually develops in acute attacks between which the person may be symptom-free, surveys analysing the frequency of this problem at any one time will provide only limited information and detailed and careful probing about previous episodes is required.

There are many different ways of performing back pain surveys. The information gathered will reflect the types of subjects studied and the information sought. This may seem obvious but serious errors have occurred by applying information gathered from a study of one group of subjects to a totally different group. To take obvious examples, a survey of back pain in children would provide very different answers from another in adults and a survey conducted in a coal-mining area would be very different from one in the stockbroker belt. We must ask whether the survey has been performed on all the people living in a particular area and whether it is a survey of the entire population, or people at work, and if the latter the type of work must be known.

The ways in which the surveys are performed also may influence the results. In industrial surveys the information that has been sought reflects the impact of back pain on work statistics, but this may give a very unreal view about the role of this problem in society at large. The number of working days lost due to back pain must be seen in relation to the type of job being performed. On the whole men do much heavier work than women but a greater prevalence of backache in men may not mean more back pain but simply that the men with perhaps the same degree of symptoms could not perform their more strenuous activities. Certain types of job cannot be performed by people with backache. If back sufferers avoided such work or rapdily left it, a survey would show a low incidence—an apparent contradiction.

Much of the information about days lost from work and the impact that the back pain problem makes upon society is derived from work records kept with varying degrees of accuracy. These results may be adequate for determining sick pay but not for the more detailed studies required for accurate statistical surveys.

The final problem is that in all the discussion in this chapter so far, I have treated back pain as a single entity. In fact we know that there are many different reasons why back pain may arise. They will be described in detail later on in this book. In determining the impact back pain makes on society it is expedient to lump them all together but this can lead to serious problems when comparing a short sharp bout of pain that is totally disabling for perhaps a few days, with a less severe chronic problem that goes on for many years.

Despite all these difficulties much useful information has been gathered. This gives some guidance as to the risks of developing back pain and its relationship to particular types of occupation. The evidence between different surveys often conflicts to a certain extent, but perhaps this is hardly surprising in view of the problems described.

Who gets back pain?

Pain in the back may develop at any age although it reaches its greatest frequency in adult life, being less frequent in younger people and also in old age. However, within the large group of disorders which may cause back pain, there are certain conditions which are more likely to develop in certain age groups. For example, bursting of an intervertebral disc—the so-called 'slipped disc'—is most frequent at about 40–45 years. On the other hand, ankylosing spondylitis usually appears in a much younger age group, commonly between 15 and 25 years. Although the frequency of back pain is relatively constant over a wide span of adult ages, the proportion of people severely disabled by back pain virtually trebles in frequency in late middle age compared with young adults. It is disturbing that recently there has been an increasing incidence of backache reported in schoolchildren. It is not clear whether this is a real increase or simply that more attention is being paid to complaints that were previously ignored. An increase in the frequency of back pain in children is unwelcome but nevertheless, it would also be of interest, as it should be relatively easy to identify the factors responsible and therefore to develop long-term solutions.

A comparison of the incidence of back pain between the sexes produces surprising results. If the survey is conducted on the whole population it has been found that back pain occurs more frequently in women than in men. The reasons for this are not at all clear. It may be that women are more prone to spinal problems. There is a suggestion that child-bearing might be responsible as we know that during pregnancy back pain may be produced because of the weight of the pregnant uterus and the increasing looseness of the spinal ligaments. However, the greatest difference between the sexes occurs in those over 50 years old, making that explanation less likely, although it remains possible that the spine has been damaged to a certain extent during pregnancy leading to problems in later life. Osteoporosis or weakening of the bones usually occurs in older people and is much more common in women than men, so explaining some of the difference. A chauvinistic suggestion is that women feel pain more readily and complain more than men; in other words they have a lower pain threshold. This suggestion inevitably arouses indignation, probably with good reason.

However, if surveys are based on industry then there is a reversal of the situation and back pain appears more frequently in men. Each year there are 627 working days lost per 1000 men at work but only 347 per 1000 women. The reason for this is that men more commonly undertake heavier work. Not only may the job lead to a greater incidence of back pain, but workers with back problems could probably continue in light work but not in heavy manual duties.

The risk of back pain is also related to one's body shape to a certain extent. There seems to be a higher incidence in those who are taller and heavier than the rest of us. As most of the body load is transmitted through the spine it seems likely that such people's backs undergo excessive stresses so that they are more readily damaged.

Although back pain usually is associated with stiffness of the spine, there is an interesting group of back sufferers whose spine, and indeed all their joints, are more flexible than normal. Such people are probably born extremely supple and remain so throughout their lives but the excessive movements which occur may eventually lead to damage and back pain. They have been described as having the 'loose-back syndrome'. Ballet dancers are known to develop wear and tear forms of arthritis and it has been thought that this is simply due to them overtaxing their joints. However, we now find that ballet dancers have excessively mobile joints. In other words they have become good dancers because their joints are so supple; the joints have not been made supple by their dancing. This suppleness, combined with the extremes of movement, can eventually lead to premature wear and tear in the joints in the same way as the loose-back syndrome.

Back pain and life-style

A constant theme in the discussion of the back pain problem is the relationship between physical work and the development of back pain. There have been striking changes in the stresses associated with daily life during man's evolution. We all constantly perform lifting and carrying movements throughout the day. A recent calculation suggested that the pre-Neolithic hunter-gatherer man only performed about 50 lifts per day whereas twentieth century man performs about ten times that figure. The current rate is also much greater than in medieval times. Whether this alone or other aspects of modern society are responsible for the present incidence of the problem is hard to say but there is good evidence indicating that stresses can be important.

Surveys within industry show that the greatest incidence of loss of work due to back pain occurs in unskilled and older workers who are required to perform physically demanding jobs. The incidence of back pain in those employed in heavy industry is some five times that in light industry. However, the information available is not entirely consistent in that there is also a high incidence in those who perform sedentary work, particularly if they spend a lot of time driving motor vehicles. The incidence of back pain is higher in nurses (17 per cent) than in policemen (6 per cent): almost equal to that in heavy industry (22 per cent). At first sight this seems surprising but the stresses involved in lifting and turning heavy patients are probably equal to those in manual work. Policemen with backache may have to retire early because they lack the physical fitness required by the Force. Olympic weight-lifters do not develop more back pain than other workers but perhaps those that do would cease to be suitable for such a competitive sport and therefore not be Olympic weight-lifters.

The trouble with industrial surveys is that they usually cover the work force as a whole and within any industry there are numerous jobs, some of which may lead to particular forms of stress, but others may not. To take an obvious example, within the coal-mining industry, the coal face workers have quite different working conditions from those engaged in transporting coal, the underground electricians, the lift men, and the surface workers. Even at the coal face there are different types of work. Detailed analyses are necessary to identify the specific factors leading to the development of back problems in the individual job.

The greater incidence of back pain in those working in heavy industry has been mentioned. However, the term 'heavy industry' covers a multitude of working conditions and the precise problems causing back pain are still being identified. Perhaps it is the increased frequency of injuries occurring in those working in such an environment that is responsible. Acute injuries, twists, or sprains are frequently reported. If a person attempts to lift an unexpectedly heavy weight then the muscles stabilizing the spine fail to provide appropriate support and may lead to damage to the back and pain. Similarly an attempt to lift an unduly heavy object whilst stooping forwards is an important risk factor. A sudden twist, particularly whilst carrying a heavy object, can be responsible. We all have countless minor twists and strains which are rapidly forgotten but in some subjects they may lead to back problems.

Major injuries to the back are much more rare. They do occur, however, and can produce fractures of the spine. Fortunately these usually heal well but occasionally they may lead to persistent pain. Apart from sudden incidents of this type it does seem that those whose jobs make the greatest demands on their back are more likely to develop back pain. In particular stooping forwards and lifting a heavy object can lead to back problems. The incidence of back pain is much less in those who stand upright or walk about. There is a somewhat high incidence in those with desk jobs. It may be that back sufferers often choose such an occupation or possibly that continuous sitting leads to weakness of the muscles supporting the spine and therefore to back pain. Certainly poor seating can aggravate the situation. Sudden jarring and vibration movements are often blamed for producing back pain. This may be why tractor drivers show a high incidence of this problem. There is a significantly increased frequency in those who are required to undertake a lot of driving in association with their work. Postmen who drive vans develop more back pain than those without driving commitments.

It therefore appears that there is a greater risk of back pain in those involved in heavy manual work. Of particular importance are jobs involving sudden and unexpected movements and prolonged stooping. Working in a poor posture, including sitting in unsuitable chairs, is a potent cause of back troubles. However, the information can be difficult to analyse and often the relationship between the back pain and work may be complicated by a compensation problem. If there is an identifiable cause that can be blamed on the job then the subject may expect some benefit. It is important to establish the facts of the matter but obviously this may colour the individual's response, either deliberately or subconsciously.

The incidence of back pain

Surveys of the frequency of backache show that it has been experienced by most of the population with very high rates in older people. However, most episodes are relatively trivial and shortlived. Medical attention is only sought in about 10 per cent of instances. Every year over 4 per cent of the population are likely to see their general practitioner because of back pain and it does seem that the frequency of seeking advice and of losing time off work for this reason is gradually increasing. The greatest risk appears between 45 and 65 years of age with between 6 and 7 per cent of all people needing medical attention. The corresponding figures are between 5 and 6 per cent for those in the 25 to 45 and 65 to 75 year age groups. In young adults between 15 and 25 years only about 2.6 per cent need medical help. In children between 5 and 15 years the figures are 2–4 per cent and under 4 years less than 1 per cent. Although rare, there is a significant problem with children which must be ignored. In general, men consult their general practitioners slightly more

often than women except in the elderly over 75 years of age when
the frequencies are reversed. This may be because elderly women
have a much greater risk of developing weak bones or osteoporosis
which is described in Chapter 11.

There has been an enormous increase in the frequency of back
pain over recent years. Indeed the figures are so dramatic that it
almost might be termed an epidemic. Figures published by the UK
Department of Health show that in 1970 about 16 million working
days were lost in Britain because of back pain but 20 years later this
figure has increased to 60 million. In other words a fourfold increase
in 20 years. In contrast if one adds up the number of working days
lost for all medical causes, in 1970 it was 314 million and now it is
455 million which is only about a 50 per cent increase. In 1970 back
pain caused only 5 per cent of the total loss of work for medical
reasons whereas 20 years later it has increased to 13 per cent. These
are frightening figures. If it goes on like this it may not be too long
before everyone is out of work because of back pain!

There are many reasons for this dramatic increase. The frequency
of back disorders may be increasing. This may be due to the lack of
physical exercise by many office workers or at the other extreme the
excessive sporting and athletic activities taken up by some. Obesity
may be putting increasing strains on the back. Work injuries may be
more common. People may be more willing to stop work because of
back pain or employers more worried about them remaining at
work in case it aggravates the problem. Social Security and
disablement benefits make it easier to have time off with backache.
Whatever the reasons, back pain is now a very common problem. It
is the most frequent cause of loss of work amongst those under the
age of 45 years and only second to heart and lung disease in older
people.

Fortunately however, most episodes of back pain are minor and
patients may not even need to see their doctor. Only about a
seventh of those who consult their general practitioner for back pain
are likely to be referred to a hospital specialist, although, by reason
of waiting list problems, many improve before they are seen. One in
six of these patients are likely to be admitted to hospital and only
one in six of these will have an operation. This means that only 0.4
per cent of people seeing their general practitioner for backache are
likely eventually to require surgery.

The community burden

The global cost of the back pain problem to our society is important in indicating the importance of the problem and the need for extra resources to be directed to improving our current treatment facilities. Around 2 000 000 adults in Great Britain consult their general practitioners each year because of the development of back pain and this problem is the cause of 6.5 per cent of general practice consultations. The average GP will see 75 new back cases per year. In total there are 3.4 million consultations per year in general practice and 0.4 million patients are seen in hospital out-patient clinics. This means that 5 per cent of all new patients attending hospital for any reason are there because of their backs; 63 000 will be admitted and 10 800 will undergo surgery.

In Great Britain in one year there were 750 000 episodes of back pain with about 60 000 000 working days lost. One in fifty of the working population lose time from work each year because of back pain. This problem accounts for nearly 10 per cent of all loss of work due to ill health and exceeds the losses due to both heart disease and bronchitis. In 1982 back pain was responsible for more than six times the number of working days lost through strikes. At any one time some 10 000 people have been off work for six months or more and 4500 for two years or more.

Economists love to quantify problems such as this in financial terms. The Office of Health Economics assessed the loss of output in Britain in 1982/83 as £1 019 million. To this should be added sickness benefits from the Social Security Fund estimated at £193 million. The health service costs include the workload on general practitioners estimated at £25.7 million, the cost of drugs at £38.9 million, the costs in providing for out-patient consultations at £25.3 million and in-patient costs, including surgery at £66.2 million. This makes the direct NHS costs total £156 million. In addition, there is an estimate of medicines and appliances bought by patients themselves thought to be anything up to £33 million.

For February 1990, the overall cost to our society was calculated as about £3 000 000 000—an absolutely staggering figure. As the back problem is still increasing, the figures are going to become worse.

Of course there may be large inaccuracies in these calculations but they represent the best estimate that we have available. Even

these figures do not attempt to assess the personal costs borne by the
pain sufferers themselves. We cannot put a figure on the value of
suffering experienced by the patient and his family. Changes of job,
modification of activities, the need for assistance, all will produce
costs and are impossible to estimate. Perhaps the wisest and least
expensive cost the back pain sufferer might choose is to purchase
this book!

Conclusions

The difficulties experienced in estimating the frequency of back pain
have been described. Despite all these and much conflicting evidence
it is clear that back pain is one of the major medical, social, and
economic problems in our society. We are beginning to identify
particular types of work associated with an increased risk of
developing back pain but as yet the limited measures that have been
taken have not led to a significant improvement in the incidence of
the problem as a whole. The need to concentrate on preventing the
development and improving the treatment of back pain is crystal
clear.

3

Discs—slipped or burst?

The phrase 'a slipped disc' is used very commonly and indeed at some time or other this diagnosis has been blamed for producing almost every form of acute back pain. There are two major errors in this. First of all discs do not and cannot slip, and secondly what does go wrong and may be called a 'slipped disc' is much less frequent than previously thought.

The correct term that should be used for patients with 'a slipped disc' is a 'herniated intervertebral disc'. What actually happens is that the disc bursts and fragments of the outer annulus fibrosus, together with some of the inner gelatinous nucleus pulposus, press on ligaments and nerves running close to the disc and produce pain (Fig. 7). The term 'slipped disc' is not only wrong but also harmful as it leads to a false idea of what is happening and therefore of the likely outcome. The mental picture produced is of a flat biscuit-like structure that slips sideways or backwards between the bones of the spine. If the disc can slip in and out in such a fashion then it could equally well slip back again and all should be well. The truth of the matter is that the disc bursts so that it is permanently damaged. Once this has happened, that disc will never be normal again. Its resistance to further injury is considerably reduced and anyone who has had a burst intervertebral disc is always at risk of further episodes of acute pain. If I could make a plea it would be for the phrase 'a slipped disc' to disappear permanently.

Although backache has been suffered by man for countless millennia and the existence of intervertebral discs has been known for many centuries, it is only very recently that the two have been put together and that the idea of disc problems producing back pain has been accepted. Before that most mechanical types of backache were blamed on strains of the various ligaments around the spine and problems with the small facet joints that lie towards the back of the vertebral column. The German pathologist, George Schmorl, had found small protrusions and leaks from the disc but did not

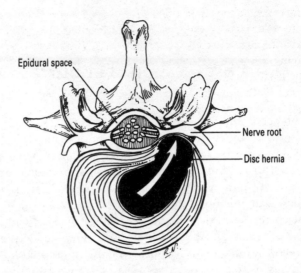

Epidural space

Nerve root

Disc hernia

Fig. 7 The disc bursts backwards and to one side pressing on the nerve root and other structures

think they were of any importance. The great advance was a study published in 1934 by two Boston surgeons, W. G. Mixter and J. S. Barr. They were treating a young man with acute back pain and for various reasons thought that it might be due to a tumour in the spine. At operation they found a swelling at the back of the disc that was compressing a nerve root. After removal of the swelling the patient was cured. When the material removed at operation was examined under microscope it was found to be lacking in cells. In contrast a tumour, and especially a cancer, would be full of cells that are dividing, so leading to growth. The material from the swelling looked very similar to that from a normal disc. When they compared the appearance with those found by Schmorl they realized that the whole problem was due to a hernia or burst of the intervertebral disc. Further examination of other similar swellings removed at operation and in the pathology collection of the Massachusetts General Hospital in Boston showed that the majority were disc bursts.

The concept that the intervertebral disc can burst and so cause back pain and sciatica had enormous appeal to orthopaedic surgeons. The reason is that if back pain were blamed on strain of the ligaments or wear and tear of the spine not much could be done for it, whereas a burst would be amenable to surgical treatment. Something constructive could be offered. The swelling was removed relieving the pressure on the damaged ligaments and nerves. Some of the disc substance was also taken away so that further leakage of material from the disc became unlikely. Following this remarkable discovery there was a tremendous surge of interest in the surgical treatment of back pain. At one time an operation was almost the standard procedure for the majority of back sufferers. The early results of surgery seemed good and for a while it seemed as if the back problem was solved. However, in recent years, and in the light of experience, we now have a very much more cautious attitude to the use of operative treatment. The natural history of many back problems is of acute episodes of pain which sooner or later get better in most people. If surgery is undertaken too readily a successful result can be confused with the natural remission that would take place anyway. Operations, however small, always carry some risk and after back surgery there is a very definite incidence of further back problems that make one cautious in advising this form of treatment. Today, surgery is reserved for those in whom there is a very clear need, where damage that can be remedied has been identified with reasonable precision, and the patient has not responded to a period of more conservative treatment. In other words operations are the last resort for certain types of back pain rather than an immediate treatment as was the case a few years ago.

What goes wrong with the disc?

Although any disc in the entire spine can herniate or burst, the most common ones to which this happens are the lowest two, that is between the fourth and fifth lumbar vertebrae and between the fifth lumbar and the top of the sacrum. Although the reasons for this are not entirely clear, the most likely explanation is that the stresses experienced by the spine are the greatest at these levels. Also the sacrum does not stand vertically but is tilted backwards, so producing a sharp curve in this region and giving a wedge shape to the discs. This wedge shape may concentrate the stresses in the back of the disc so making these lower lumbar discs particularly liable to damage.

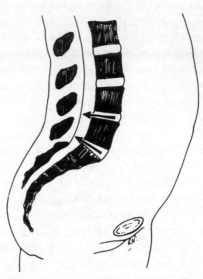

Fig. 8 Backwards bursts of the discs between the fourth and fifth lumbar vertebrae, and between the fifth lumbar and first sacral vertebrae

Briefly, in disc herniation, the disc ruptures or bursts so that debris from the disc protrudes and can damage the surrounding structures. Most commonly these ruptures occur at the back of the disc but to one side or the other. These are known technically as the posterolateral edges of the disc. Sometimes, however, the burst may occur directly backwards in the midline and this is known as a central posterior hernia. The direction the burst takes, together with the anatomical arrangement of surrounding structures, will determine the amount of damage that is produced and the type of symptoms that arise.

The backs of the vertebral bodies and the intervertebral discs are sheathed by tough fibrous material known as the posterior longitudinal ligament and this contains numerous tiny nerves. Interestingly, in the substance of the disc itself there are no nerves except at the outer margin where it is attached to the surrounding ligaments. The principal site where the nerve fibres are concentrated is at the back of the disc at the attachment of the ligament running up the backs of the vertebral bodies. It is likely that the acute pain felt in the back, which occurs when the disc bursts or herniates is due to this burst occurring backwards and usually to one or other side affecting this ligament and the concentration of nerve fibres (Fig. 7). Behind the ligament are the nerve roots which have separated from the spinal cord and are sweeping down through the vertebral canal to emerge through the openings between the vertebrae known as the intervetebral foramina. The material from the burst disc may breach the posterior longitudinal ligament and damage these nerve roots. A small burst may only damage one root whereas a larger one, particularly if it is towards the midline, may affect several. The damage to the nerve root will produce unpleasant sensations of pain, numbness, and tingling which are felt in the area that particular root supplies. In other words the pain will generally be felt in the lower limb. The damage may also interfere with the transmission of impulses down the nerve to motivate the muscles and this may cause weakness of particular movements. Some of the nerve roots also supply the bladder and the lower bowel. Damage here may lead to loss of control of passing urine and motions and sometimes to incontinence. When this occurs it is a major emergency and this is perhaps the only reason for immediate surgery for a prolapse. It is essential to relieve the pressure on these particular nerve roots as soon as possible in order to avoid permanent damage.

Why does the disc burst?

Use of the back, particularly heavy lifting, increases the pressure in the disc. An obvious explanation for what happens when the disc bursts would be that this pressure exceeds the strength of the outer annulus. Although this mechanism seems so simple and perhaps obvious, we now believe that this is not the whole story and that in most cases discs that burst were previously damaged before the actual burst has occurred.

Many episodes of disc rupture occur after quite trivial stresses— the sorts of stresses that we all undergo without noticing them. Some patients develop acute back pain after lifting a book, or twisting round, or perhaps mowing the lawn. It is difficult to believe that such forces are enough to produce a burst, but the changes in the spines of such people are the same as those occurring in other patients after damage by heavier loads.

For obvious reasons we are not able deliberately to subject human beings to loads to see what happens to the discs. However, although it seems a bit macabre, studies have been made of the spines of people who have died from accidents after sudden vertical forces on their spines. The most frequent cause of this is in people who receive fatal parachuting injuries when they land on their bottoms. The enormous forces experienced by their discs do not make the outer annulus of the intervertebral disc fail and do not produce the types of burst that are found in our patients. Examination of the spines have shown that if the forces are great enough, the vertebral end-plates give way, but the annulus fibrosus remains intact.

Another approach to the problem has been to examine spines from people who have died from unrelated causes and subject them to forces and observe how the disc will fail when tested to the extreme. Such studies have been performed in several different ways but in general they show that the normal disc is so strong that it is the bony vertebral end-plate that gives way rather than the annulus fibrosus. Except under special circumstances, force alone is not enough to produce a burst intervertebral disc. Further studies indicate that it is those discs that were previously abnormal that will rupture in a way that resembles the burst occurring in life. The disc is already weakened by fissures, cracks, or degeneration and the stress experienced is merely the final event in making the disc burst.

The reasons for weakness or damage of the disc, placing it at risk of herniation, are uncertain. One suggested cause is fatigue failure due to repetitive stresses similar to metal fatigue and failure after constant bending and straightening. The discs in different people differ in shape and in some the forces may become concentrated at a weak point, so gradually leading towards permanent damage.

These conclusions are clearly controversial because they have important medico-legal implications. If a person develops a rupture of an intervertebral disc while at work, it is possible the disc was about to burst anyway as it was already weakened and damaged. The action that produced the rupture was merely the final incident making the burst occur, not the basic cause. Under such circumstances there is now some doubt about whether the accident was totally responsible for the prolapse and therefore whether compensation is fully justifiable.

Symptoms

Although rupture of an intervertebral disc can occur at almost any age it is most frequent between 20 and 50 years and the peak incidence is between 40 and 45 years. It affects not only those involved in heavy manual work but also those who perform sedentary work who suddenly take unaccustomed exercise, for example office workers who spend their day at a desk and their evenings watching the television and who attack the garden or perform vigorous exercise at the weekend.

Some patients may have noticed warning symptoms over the few days prior to the hernia. There may be aches and pains and stiffness in the back which herald the acute episode. The actual incident that precipitates the pain may be quite trivial, such as a sudden twist or bending forward to pick something up. The pain may strike immediately or it may develop gradually over a few minutes or a couple of hours. When it starts suddenly it is felt in the back and only later spreads down the lower limb. It may be so sudden that it feels like being struck and in Germany this has been called *hexenschuss*: a witch's blow. The pain may be so bad that the sufferer is unable to straighten up and finds himself stuck in the bent position and in great agony.

At first this pain is felt in the lower back in the midline or to one or other side. Because this acute attack of pain occurs in the lumbar region it is sometimes called 'acute lumbago'. After a while, maybe several hours, the pain spreads down the leg and may ease up in the back. This spreading into the leg occurs because the material that has burst out from the disc compresses and stretches the nerve root, and the area where pain is felt depends upon the particular nerve root involved (Fig. 2). Commonly the pain is down the back of the thigh, the back or outside of the lower leg, and the outer edge and sometimes the top of the foot. There is also a sensation of numbness and tingling. Some people find it very difficult to identify the area where the pain is felt but find it easier to describe the site of tingling. The doctor will wish to know exactly where these abnormal sensations are felt as they help to tell him which particular nerve root is affected. These acute symptoms are made worse by straining, coughing, and sneezing, because these activities will raise the pressure within the vertebral canal adding slightly to the stress on the nerves.

The nerve roots that may be damaged by a burst joint together in a complicated combination to form the sciatic nerve which runs down the back of the thigh to supply the lower limb. This is why the pain down the back of the leg is known as 'sciatica'. Sciatica can be agonizingly severe and may be made worse by movement and exercise.

It is rare for the nerves to the bladder and lower bowel to be affected but if they are there may be some loss of the normal sensations on passing urine and motions. Incontinence and soiling of the underclothes may occur. There may also be loss of ability to feel and a sensation of numbness in the saddle area. As already mentioned this is an emergency which requires immediate investigations and treatment.

The doctor's examination

The medical examination reveals various features which help the doctor to make the appropriate diagnosis. The patient is in pain and a simple look at the face will often indicate the severity of the problem. He may lie curled up or flat unwilling to move for fear of making things worse. The back itself may not be straight but may show a sharp twist, which is know technically as a 'scoliosis'. This occurs because the muscles on either side of the spine contract hard into spasm and pull the spine sideways. It is a reflex attempt by the body to twist the spine so as to relieve the pressure in the damaged area. It is possible to feel the muscles on either side of the spine and to detect the unequal muscle contraction. The doctor will watch the patient trying to move his back and will see that certain movements are virtually impossible whereas others may be relatively free. Bending forwards and to one side is most often limited whereas moving in the other directions is relatively little affected.

By careful palpation of the back, it is sometimes possible to identify areas that are particularly tender and pressure may make the symptoms worse. This form of examination can give a crude idea of where the problem is but sometimes it may be inaccurate as the back pain and tenderness may be a little way from the actual site of the problem.

The lower limbs will be carefully examined to detect evidence of nerve damage. An important examination is the straight-leg-raising test (Fig. 9). The patient lies on his back and the doctor raises the ankle as far as possible with the knee held out straight. In a normal person it is possible to bend the hip in this way between 70° and 90°. However, in patients with sciatica straight-leg-raising makes the symptoms very much worse so that the movement becomes severely restricted. Some patients can tolerate only 10° of movement. Straight-leg-raising stretches the sciatic nerve and pulls on the nerve roots, stressing them that little bit more and therefore exacerbating the symptoms. Straight-leg-raising improves as the back problem gets better and measurement of this movement is commonly used to follow the progress of the patient with treatment.

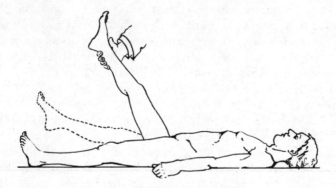

Fig. 9 The straight-leg-raising test

The doctor will examine the power of various muscles in the leg. He will test the reflexes, particularly the knee jerk and the ankle jerk, and he will look for loss of ability to feel sensations in the leg. With knowledge of the areas supplied by the various nerve roots he may then be able to work out which particular one has been damaged.

It is fortunate indeed that the vast majority of attacks of back pain and sciatica due to a burst of an intervertebral disc will get better spontaneously. With appropriate rest and treatment the symptoms gradually remit, often within a few days but sometimes requiring a much longer period. The treatment of acute back pain and sciatica will be described in Chapter 5. If the symptoms fail to improve, then further and more detailed investigations will be required.

Investigations that may be performed

In the patient with a straightforward burst intervertebral disc, acute low back pain, and sciatica, the diagnosis is obvious and further tests may not be necessary. Blood tests and X-rays need be performed only if there is some doubt about the diagnosis, or if the symptoms fail to get better and some further action is being considered. Briefly, all the usual blood tests should show normal results. Rupture of the disc does not affect the blood, so these tests are helpful only in checking whether some other condition may be present.

Ordinary X-rays of the back are equally uninformative. When we look at an X-ray we examine the shadows produced by structures interfering with a beam of X-rays falling on photographic film. Bones are relatively dense in contrast with soft tissues such as flesh so that a clear picture is seen and an abnormality in the bone, such as a fracture, is obvious. The intervertebral disc is made up of soft tissues which cast extremely faint shadows and cannot be seen in the spine because of the very dense surrounding bone of the vertebral column. For this reason it is not possible to see the bulge of the disc due to the burst. In the patient with an acute prolapsed disc the X-ray may appear normal, other than perhaps showing the twist of the spine due to the sciatic scoliosis. However, the disc has lost some of its substance and further X-rays taken months or years later may show some loss of height of the disc and wear and tear changes of the surrounding vertebrae. This is one cause of the wear and tear changes, which are known as lumbar spondylosis and will be described in the next chapter.

More sophisticated techniques are available which are used to pick out the damaged disc and to show the burst. Some methods are 'invasive', that is they involve special injections into the spine. They can be somewhat unpleasant and therefore they are reserved for those few patients in whom there are special problems, particularly those for whom an operation is being considered.

One technique involves injection of a special fluid that is opaque to X-rays directly into the vertebral canal. This fluid will occupy the space immediately behind the vertebral bodies and intervertebral discs. If there is any obstruction it will block the flow of this dye so that a space appears on the X-ray. By this means it is possible to 'see' the burst accurately. Until recently, the material injected was an oily fluid and the technique was known as myelography. Because this fluid was very thick, a bit like treacle, it failed to provide as much detail as may be gained from newer X-ray techniques. Moreover, on occasions the oily material persisted in the spine indefinitely. Sometimes attempts were made to withdraw the oil following the X-ray examination but in general it was impossible to remove it completely and the remaining dye can still be seen in X-rays of the back taken many years later. Unfortunately, the dye itself can lead to problems and in particular to chronic inflammation and scarring in the arachnoid and dural coats around the nerve roots. The problems due to arachnoiditis are described in Chapter 8. The numbers of patients who develop this problem as a result of having had this particular test are few but it has been responsible for some very severe and persistent back pain cases.

Because of dissatisfaction with the quality of views obtained using the oily dye and the risk of developing arachnoiditis, we now prefer a new fluid which is watery in consistency rather than oily. This dye only lasts in the spine for a few hours and then is cleared away by the blood. This means that the long-term problems are avoided and at the same time this new technique provides a very much better quality X-ray and much more detail of the nerve roots. The technique using this new fluid is known as radiculography.

There are some newer methods used in X-ray departments which are only available in special centres. One of the most promising is discography in which the radio-opaque fluid is injected directly into the intervertebral disc, using X-ray television to guide the direction of the needle. The examination is carried out under local anaesthetic. Not only does the method show if the disc is normal or not, but also injection of the disc that has burst and is responsible for the patient's symptoms will actually reproduce the problem during the time of the injection. In this way the disc that is at fault can be precisely identified.

Computers for investigation of the spine

In the last few years there has been a revolution in the techniques for obtaining accurate pictures of the inside of the spine. We are now using computers to analyse X-rays and are able to detect details which previously were totally inaccessible.

The CAT scan refers to the Computerized Axial Tomographic scan and was a method invented by Geoffrey Hounsfield, an engineer working for EMI in Hayes, Middlesex. He shared the Nobel Prize for this development. It has revolutionized many X-ray techniques and is particularly useful for brain disorders. The method involves passing a beam of X-rays through the body and recording the transmitted signal on the other side. The beam and the recorder are rotated around the part being studied and the information received is processed in a computer. By making an extraordinary number of complex calculations, the computer will build up and reconstruct a picture of a horizontal section across the human body. This is a vertical view of a section of the spine that is impossible to obtain using conventional X-rays. When this technique is applied to the human spine it is possible to see the size and shape of the vertebral canal and recognize when it is abnormal (Plates 1, 2, and 3). In the early CAT scan machines, not enough detail was provided to see a burst of the intervertebral disc but the latest generation of models are now so sophisticated that a prolapse can be recognized without the need to inject dye into the vertebral canal. At the present time, the accuracy of the CAT scan is broadly similar to that of radiculography but, in the long run, with the speed of developments that are taking place, it seems virtually certain that the CAT scan will sooner or later provide better information about damage to the disc. Unfortunately the apparatus to undertake this test is extremely expensive; however, it is becoming generally available and much more widely used.

There is now an even more exciting development which is known as magnetic resonance imaging or MRI. Atoms consist of electrons spinning round a nucleus and in doing so they generate a magnetic field. If they are placed within another magnetic field they will alter the balance of the magnetic field so that they produce a signal that can be measured. This signal is analysed using a computer in a similar way to CAT scanning and images are produced which can provide very fine detail of the inside of the spine. This MRI technique has a number of advantages over CAT scanning. In the first place it does not involve exposure to any X-rays so that the risk produced by radiation, which admittedly is very small, is here completely avoided. The quality of the picture provided seems better than that obtained by CAT scanning and in particular it allows a detailed reconstruction of a vertical slice through the skeleton so that disc degeneration (Plate 4) and bulges at the back of the disc can be easily identified (Plate 5). This can be achieved by CAT scans but MRI produces much better images. Finally, the MRI technique can tell us about the actual chemical structure within the spine and the intervertebral disc whereas the CAT scan only shows the density of X-rays. Using MRI we can now recognize the earliest stages of disc degeneration and perhaps in the future it may allow us to predict those discs which are likely to herniate.

We know that CAT scanning is expensive; however, unfortunately MRI is vastly more expensive still. The patient is placed within extremely strong magnetic fields and in order to generate these fields very powerful electromagnets are used. Enormous currents are required and in the normal way these would require a phenomenal power supply. An important property of electrical conduction is that resistance to electric currents virtually disappears at extremely low temperatures near absolute zero which is—273° C. This property is used in magnetic resonance imaging so that by super-cooling the coils inside the electromagnets sufficiently large electric currents may be obtained and circulated virtually indefinitely without the need for the enormous power supply. However, in order to obtain super-cooling the coils have to be bathed in liquid helium. This is very expensive and evaporates very rapidly so that the liquid helium, in turn, is surrounded by a layer of liquid nitrogen, which is very much cheaper and reduces the rapid evaporation of the helium. The result is that the magnetic resonance apparatus, the running costs, and in particular the provision of liquid helium and nitrogen together with extremely skilled technical support make this type of investigation extremely expensive. Magnetic resonance imaging is becoming more widely available but it is likely that it will always be the preserve of specialist centres and never become a simple routine investigation.

4

Mechanical problems and backache

The spine is such a complex mechanical structure that it is hardly surprising that many things may go wrong. The most well known of these is the slipped disc, which should be called the burst or herniated disc. This has been dealt with at length in the previous chapter. However, there are many other mechanical problems that may arise in the spine and which actually occur much more frequently than a burst disc. In some of these the cause is obvious but in others it may be not clear and the symptoms are not severe enough to require the ultimate diagnostic test, namely surgery and examination of the offending part. In such cases the characteristics of the problem indicate some mechanical cause and usually some idea of its nature. It is not uncommon, however, for the experts to disagree on the precise fault as well as how it is best treated. Recent research combined with the use of advanced technology for diagnosis is helping to elucidate some of these very difficult problems.

Wear and tear in the spine

The spine of the young differs from that of the elderly. It is supple and flexible rather than stiff and rigid. The intervertebral disc is a springy cushion with a jelly-like centre but with age it becomes tough and fibrous with a reduction in its vertical height. The disc loses its ability to transmit forces in the optimum fashion and restricts the amount of movement allowed between the adjacent vertebrae. At the same time the bony surfaces above and below the discs, the vertebral end-plates, also show wear and tear changes. The surfaces of the bone become thickened and a rim of bone develops around the edge of the disc (Fig. 10). This is an automatic attempt by the body to splint the spine and to prevent further damage. These changes in and around the intervertebral discs are called spondylosis and in the low back are therefore known as lumbar spondylosis. Degenerative changes can also affect the small facet joints that lie behind and on either side of the vertebral canal. These joints are synovial joints—that is they contain a fluid-filled space with gliding cartilage surfaces and are similar in principle although not in detail to the joints in the limbs. Wear and tear in these joints is known as osteoarthritis. The cartilage becomes soft and can break up and its surface is worn away. The bone near the joint surfaces becomes thickened, especially around the rims of the facet joints, so adding to the splinting effect.

Although spondylosis and osteoarthritis are described separately they usually occur together so that it is difficult to distinguish the effects of one from the other. Wear and tear changes in the spine are remarkably common. They become much more frequent as we get older. This does not mean that the young are immune, however. The earliest changes may appear in the 20–30 year age group but at this age they are of course relatively mild. Commonly the disc shows early signs of wear and tear but the bones are not yet affected. The result is that the X-rays look normal at this stage although these early changes can be seen on an MRI scan. Later on the wear and tear changes become more frequent and severe. By the age of 60 almost everybody has some wear and tear changes in the spine which may be recognized on X-rays. They are so common that one must wonder if it is right to call them abnormal. If everyone develops spondylosis and osteoarthritis, surely that is 'normal' and the man whose spine remains as it was in his youth must be abnormal!

These wear and tear changes are diagnosed from X-rays of the back. It is relatively easy to see the spaces occupied by the discs on the X-rays but the facet joints are much more difficult to identify. For this reason the diagnosis of osteoarthritis in the lumbar area is much less reliable than that of spondylosis. Even X-rays that show the changes in the discs are not as good as one might think. The disc itself is not opaque to X-rays and quite severe wear and tear in the disc substance may develop and yet the X-rays appear virtually normal. In my own studies of discs I found that the most trivial changes on X-rays could indicate gross damage to the disc.

Wear and tear does not affect all the discs in the lumbar region similarly. It is far more frequent in the lower two lumbar discs than in the upper three. This probably is due to the greater loads experienced by the low back and also the tilt backwards of the sacrum or tail bone so creating unequal stresses in various parts of the vertebrae and discs connected to it.

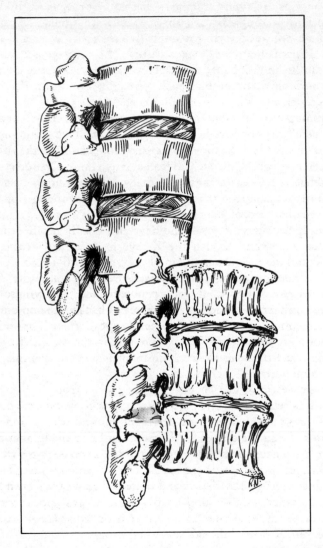

Fig. 10 The vertebrae in a normal spine and in one showing spondylosis with degenerative changes around the intervertebral discs and in the facet joints

As these wear and tear changes occur so frequently we might infer that they are the cause of back pain, and the reason backache is so common. If every older person has lumbar spondylosis and osteoarthritis, we should all suffer from back pain sooner or later. As these changes are permanent, we should then have pain all the time. Fortunately this is far from the case but these points present the nub of the problem. Backache is common and these changes are common. However, in surveys in which the incidence of backache was compared with the frequency of wear and tear of the spine on X-ray, it was found that, although backache was more frequent in those with the worst X-rays, compared with those with normal or nearly normal X-rays the difference in frequency was remarkably small. Those with the grossest changes had only a 12 per cent higher incidence of back pain than those with the best X-rays. This must mean that in the majority of people wear and tear changes found by X-rays are not responsible for back pain.

This point has enormous significance but is often missed in ordinary clinical practice. A patient gets backache, an X-ray is taken and shows these wear and tear changes, and lo and behold the diagnosis is made. It is not nearly as easy as that. Many people with such changes do not have a back problem and if the symptoms are blamed on them other important causes of backache sooner or later will be missed. Simply finding these changes on X-rays is not enough. The clinical problems due to wear and tear of the spine are poorly defined; the symptoms and the findings on examination are not unique for this condition and may occur for other reasons. This adds to the confusion.

Why is it then that one back with wear and tear changes can be very painful yet another with apparently the same degree of damage seen on X-rays is pain free. Again wear and tear damage on X-rays is permanent yet many patients with such damage have long years without pain and only occasional acute episodes. This suggests that the wear and tear changes do not directly lead to back pain but to other forms of damage, perhaps to ligaments and tendons. Recent research indicates that wear and tear problems may damage the blood vessels around the nerves and lead to the development of scar tissue. Scar tissue leads to the symptoms and as the secondary changes come and go so the back pain passes through phases of exacerbation and remissions. Our current understanding of this problem is described in Chapter 8.

This makes for scepticism about the value of X-rays of the back. Commonly patients with backache expect an X-ray to be taken and will feel dissatisfied with their doctor if one is not ordered. However, when the routine examination and blood test indicate nothing untoward, studies show that the X-ray does not make any useful contribution to the diagnosis or treatment. All X-irradiation is harmful, the amount of risk depending on the dose of X-rays. Taking an X-ray of the low back requires quite a high dose with a small but definite risk to the ovaries in women and the testes in men. It is possible to protect these organs to a great extent but it is far better to avoid unnecessary X-rays.

Commonly, symptoms due to lumbar spondylosis and osteo-arthritis develop as one gets older and produce aching and stiffness in the lower back. The symptoms are often intermittent with good and bad periods and sometimes the back can feel quite normal between attacks. Pain is felt in the back but may spread into the buttocks and sometimes down the thighs. Posture seems all-important in producing symptoms. Bending forwards, and par-ticularly lifting heavy weights, sitting in a poor chair, and sleeping on a soft mattress all make things worse. It is usually possible to find a position of comfort and most patients find that standing upright or sitting with the back properly supported will provide relief. These points are dealt with in more detail in Chapters 5 and 9. The symptoms in the back are made worse by exercise and on the whole are easier after rest, although some patients seize up and take a minute or two to get going after prolonged inactivity.

The most obvious feature of the back with lumbar spondylosis and osteoarthritis is loss of its ability to move. There is stiffness on bending forwards and backwards and attempts at these movements can make the pain worse. Sometimes bending or twisting the back sideways may also be restricted although generally these move-ments are relatively unaffected. There is one form of degenerative change in the back which may be so widespread that the whole spine becomes stiff and then all movement is lost. Interestingly though, this is not usually a painful condition. Movement of a damaged joint causes pain. When the spine is completely rigid there is no pain.

Some back sufferers can identify the part of their back which is the most painful and careful feeling may show that it is tender. This palpation technique can indicate the particular region of the spine which is responsible for the symptoms. However, it is not always accurate because of the complex ways in which the nerves supplying the spine itself combine with one another. The symptoms and tenderness can be at an area quite different from that actually responsible for the problem.

All this indicates that the whole concept of wear and tear in the spine producing backache is unsatisfactory. Undoubtedly it is responsible in some people but its presence can be misleading in others.

Fractures

A broken bone in the arm or leg is extremely painful. The fracture is rested in a sling or in a plaster-of-Paris cast and gradually it will heal. New bone grows across the break and connects the two ends, eventually to form a solid structure again. At the same time the severe pain during the fracture improves. If the two broken bone ends are not properly held but are free to move against each other severe pain will be felt and healing will be delayed. With appropriate splinting the improvements in symptoms is much more rapid and healing enhanced.

Precisely the same type of problem can affect the back. A major accident can cause a fracture of the spine. Most often there is crushing of one of the vertebral bodies. Patients with weak bones, osteoporosis (Chapter 11), are particularly at risk of spinal fractures which may follow quite trivial stress. Following a fracture there will be very severe pain in the back and the patient will be scared to move for fear of making the pain worse. At its worst these fractures may damage the spinal cord or nerve roots. Paraplegia, or paralysis of the legs, following an accident to the spine, develops in this way. With rest the fractured vertebra will gradually heal, although the back never regains its former shape, and the back pain will usually get better. The evidence of the injury can be seen on X-rays for life.

Such gross fractures as these are obvious and fortunately are uncommon. We now know however, that much smaller fractures may occur and actually are quite frequent. They are difficult to recognize on X-rays and that is why the diagnosis is so often missed. Small fractures may occur in the vertebral arches at the back of the spinal column. This is because these parts of the spine normally transmit a very large proportion of the total force and this is enormously increased by bending the spine backwards. Examination of this part of the spine by X-ray is very difficult. The detail is not clear and tiny fractures of this sort are easily missed. Only special X-ray techniques provide the clarity of detail required and even by using the most up-to-date methods it is likely that many cases are missed. I have seen patients with acute back pain that developed following some excessive exertion. The special X-rays showed the tiny fracture. After a few days' rest the pain improved; subsequent X-rays showed the healing of the fracture site. There must be many people with acute back pain for this reason in whom the symptoms are blamed on damage to the ligaments or other structures or on wear and tear of the spine.

Bone is not a uniform material but consists of a thick outer coat containing within it a meshwork of filaments known as trabeculae. These trabeculae are very thin threads of bone and form the inner framework of the whole structure. Between them lie the blood-forming cells of the bone marrow. Fractures of these tiny trabeculae are quite common. They are so small that they are known as micro-fractures. Often they occur close to the vertebral end-plates where stresses are concentrated. Overloading the spine can produce a micro-fracture and severe pain just as any other fracture would. With rest the fracture site heals and the pain gets better. Unfortunately, the X-ray techniques available today will not provide enough detail of these trabeculae, so we have no method of diagnosing these micro-fractures in life. Advances may make this possible in the future.

Vertebral slips

The vertebrae sit one on top of another, forming a column. Normally these vertebrae remain in place but sometimes one vertebra may slip forwards or backwards on the one below. A forward slip is known as a spondylolisthesis and a backward slip as a retrolisthesis. There are two main ways in which the spine becomes unstable in this way. One is a break in the bony arch at the back of the vertebra so that the stabilizing action of the elements at the back of the spine is lost. Until recently it was thought that these breaks occurred because the arch had not developed properly during

childhood. However, we now believe that most occur due to a
fracture following injury. This fails to heal, so leaving the spine
unstable. The second mechanism is wear and tear of the spine,
which can also allow the vertebrae to slip. With spondylosis,
excessive movement appears between the vertebrae and the slip
develops.

The patient with a vertebral slip suffers from back pain because of
damage to the spinal ligaments. The nerve roots become stretched at
the site of the slip so that problems develop in the lower limbs.
Naturally, symptoms are made worse by moving the back. The
diagnosis is made from the X-rays.

Increased mobility

Some of us are more supple than others. It is this characteristic
which distinguishes good dancers and sportsmen from the rest of
us. At first sight this increased mobility would seem to be an
advantage but in certain conditions it can be carried to an extreme
and then be a real handicap.

There are certain medical disorders of looseness of the supporting
tissues of the body. The principal ones are known as Ehlers–Danlos
and Marfan's syndromes. People with these disorders may have
such loose joints that they can twist and bend them in ways not
available to the rest of us. Certain forms of these conditions produce
the 'India-rubber men' that we see in the circus. This looseness of
the tissues can affect other structures besides the joints and
sometimes lead to internal damage. In most people being loose-
jointed or 'double-jointed' does not carry any risk of internal
problems. However, such people are at risk of damaging their joints
very easily and eventually may develop premature wear and tear
changes.

Ballet dancers have very supple joints. Girls become ballet
dancers because they are born with joints more supple than normal
rather than the other way round, although practising exercises
which make the joints more supple obviously helps. Even joints
used in exercises and dancing are found to be much more flexible
than normal in ballet dancers, who have a greater risk of wear and
tear damage to their joints than the rest of us. It seems that the
excessive stresses to which they subject their joints is responsible.
The same sort of problem can also occur in footballers. A good

footballer has more supple joints than normal so that he can twist
and turn with a fluency that is beyond most people. Those
footballers who are more supple are at greater risk of damaging their
joints in the long run.

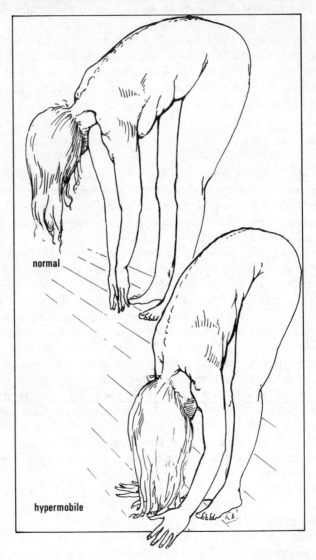

Fig. 11 Normal and hypermobile backs

Similar problems occur in the back. Some of us have excessively flexible spines. A useful test is to try and touch your toes with your legs straight. Most of us can almost or just about get there but the hypermobile person will not only get there but can even place the palms of his hands flat on the floor (Fig. 11). This excessive movement can lead to premature wear and tear damage in the spine and recurrent back pain, a problem which has been called the 'loose-back syndrome'. Back pain develops, particularly on movement. The physician can be very surprised at the excellent mobility of the back despite such severe back symptoms and it is all too easy to minimize a patient's complaint or even to state the patient is 'neurotic'. Many of these back sufferers feel frustrated because of their impression that their medical advisers do not believe that they have such severe problems. Understanding by the physician of the nature of this type of problem reassures the back sufferer as well as leading towards constructive advice and treatment.

Abnormal mobility can develop in another way. If for any reason one section of the spine is stiff there may be excessive movement above or below this segment in order to compensate for it. We often find that this excessive movement in one localized region leads to severe degenerate changes and symptoms at that level. The pain is produced not by the stiff segment itself but by the compensating excessive movement that is associated with it. Observation of the back can sometimes show which areas move normally and which abnormally but generally the diagnosis is made from X-rays. In order to diagnose this problem properly the X-rays are sometimes taken with the spine both bent forwards and backwards, to show the full range of movements.

Narrowing of the vertebral canal—spinal stenosis

As explained previously, the nerve roots pass down through the vertebral canal and emerge through openings at the sides of the spinal column known as the intervertebral foramina. Canals vary considerably in size and shape between different people. In most of us the canal is quite large but in some it is relatively small so that the nerve roots are much more tightly packed. The shape of the canal may also be changed. The intervertebral foramen through which the

nerve roots emerge from the spine, can become very narrow so that
the nerve may be trapped and squashed (Fig. 12).

As a result of the reduction in size of the vertebral canal, any
protrusion into it will inevitably injure the nerve root, whereas if

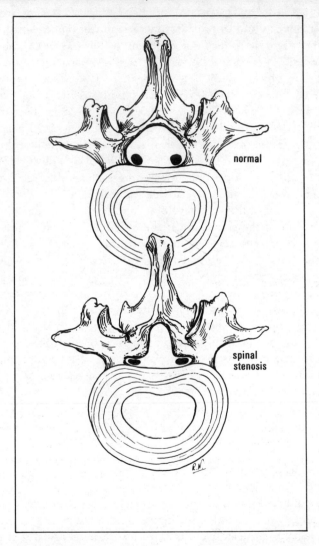

Fig. 12 Spine canal shapes—normal and spinal stenosis

there was an open canal it would merely push the nerve aside without causing damage. This narrowing of the vertebral canal is known as spinal stenosis. It is quite common, occurring in about 15 per cent of the population. The problem arises due to a combination of the shape of the canal having simply grown that way and also bony thickening around the margins of the disc and the facet joints in degenerative disease reducing the canal dimensions.

Anyone with spinal stenosis is at additional risk of developing back pain from an intrusion into the canal space. People who develop sciatica due to a burst intervetebral disc have smaller canals than normal. They were at risk because of their vertebral canal size. If they had a larger canal, the burst disc would probably not have led to serious back problems.

There are two characteristic patterns of symptoms associated with spinal stenosis. The first is due to the small size of the vertebral canal—central stenosis, and the second to narrowing of the intervertebral foramen—foraminal stenosis (Plates 2 and 3).

In central stenosis the patient develops low back pain with numbness, tingling, and painful cramps in the lower limbs. These occur on exercise and may develop after walking several hundred yards or less. Sometimes they are sufficiently severe to force the patient to stop and rest. After 5 or 10 minutes the pain gradually gets better. This pattern of symptoms is often confused with 'intermittent claudication'—painful cramps developing in the calf due to an obstructed blood supply to the leg. In claudication the symptoms develop on walking and are relieved by rest in a similar but not identical fashion. When the pain is due to spinal stenosis, the blood supply to the leg and in particular the pulses in the feet are normal.

The physical dimensions of the vertebral canal are slightly larger when the spine is bent forwards than when it is bent backwards. Because of this the pain may be easier if prevented by flexing forwards. This accounts for the curious phenomenon experienced by patients who find that walking produces the symptoms whereas they are able to cycle for longer periods without any pain. They walk with their spines upright but cycle with them bent. Some patients find they can walk upstairs with no difficulty but develop pain on walking downstairs. This may seem odd, but it is because they walk upstairs with the spine bent slightly forwards and downstairs with it arched backwards.

These two features, pain developing on walking and relieved by bending forwards produce another curious habit practised by many of these patients. After walking perhaps a few hundred yards they crouch down to do up a shoe lace. They then walk on again, then stop and repeat with the other shoe. They may do this again. The reason is that they stop to rest for a few minutes because of pain developing in the leg, crouching down bends the spine and helps to relieve the pain and by appearing to do up a shoe lace they avoid any embarrassment.

In foraminal stenosis, pain, numbness, and tingling develop in one or other leg. There is a superficial resemblance to sciatica due to a burst intervertebral disc but with some important differences. The pain is present constantly and may still continue while the subject is at rest and even in bed in contrast with the usual relief in sciatica due to a herniated disc. The straight-leg-raising test can be normal in patients with this problem whereas there is restriction of straight-leg-raising when the problem is a herniated disc. The reason is that the burst disc will displace the nerve root and stretch it so that it cannot accommodate any further tension. In foraminal stenosis the nerve root is squashed but not stretched so that there is less likelihood of the straight-leg-raising manœuvre aggravating the symptoms.

Sometimes however, the clinical problems are not as clear cut as those described and we now know that narrowing of the canal increases the risks of development of other types of back pain. It is important to make the diagnosis as it can be quite easy to reduce the pressure on the nerve roots by operation. Unfortunately it is difficult to determine the size and shape of the canal by ordinary tests. X-rays taken from front to back or from side to side will give only very limited information. A vertical view of the vertebral canal is needed, but it is not possible to obtain such a view using simple X-ray techniques. For this reason there has been enormous interest in the newer technologies which have been adapted to solving this particular problem.

The best method is the CAT scan (Chapter 3). It provides an excellent view of the shape of the vertebral canal and will clearly demonstrate bony swelling from the vertebral bodies and facet joints into the canal which may lead to the spinal stenosis problem (Plates 2 and 3).

Other abnormalities of development of the spine

No two spines are identical and the range of differences can be enormous. Normally five lumbar vertebrae sit on top of the sacrum. On occasions there may only be four with the last lumbar vertebra actually jointed into the sacral bone. In others there may be six lumbar vertebrae, the first part of the sacrum being free and appearing as an additional lumbar vertebra. There are other variations in which the spine appears inadequately formed in a somewhat abnormal shape.

These and other developmental changes are common and in general do not produce any back pain. It is important not to blame backache on them too readily. The only time such abnormalities of development can give rise to trouble is if they alter the mobility of associated parts of the spine and lead to premature wear and tear changes.

Other abnormalities of development occur during adolescence. In Scheuermann's osteochondritis there is a developmental abnormality in the intervertebral discs and in the surfaces of the vertebral bodies that are in contact with them. This particularly affects the vertebrae in the back of the chest and may produce premature wear and tear changes and the development of a forward stoop known as a kyphosis. It may be associated with an aching pain in the back of the chest and more persistent pain in later life. Exercises and careful attention to posture are important in order to prevent the stoop developing. Another developmental problem is a twist in the spine known as a scoliosis. This starts in adolescence and if not properly treated on occasions can lead to a severe deformity. The cause is uncertain but it seems likely to be an imbalance of the muscular control of the spine during the formative years. Expert advice is required in order to decide how to prevent progress of the scoliosis and to correct it if severe.

The various types of non-specific back pain

The difficulties in deciding on the true diagnosis in this very large group of back problems have already been mentioned. There are many people with constant or recurrent backache, perhaps exacerbated by stooping and sometimes with acute episodes but who are relatively well between attacks of pain. The characteristics of the symptoms and findings on examination may suggest a mechanical cause but the diagnostic terms that are used are often very unsatisfactory. It is particularly this group that produces much of the confusion in our understanding of the whole back problem. Some of these patients have X-ray changes indicating wear and tear of the spine but it has already been mentioned how difficult it is to ascertain the true significance of such features. The ultimate test, examination of the tissues, is rarely if ever possible as an operation is hardly ever required.

With the doubts that exist about the true diagnosis it is better to label these problems as 'non-specific back pain'. This term indicates back pain of uncertain cause but with any serious disorder excluded. This is an honest appraisal of our understanding and avoids deluding both the patient and the doctor that the cause of the pain is properly understood. Within the whole group of non-specific back pains, we can now pick out various entities with varying degrees of certainty or uncertainty but so often the problem is confusing with the same patient being given a variety of diagnoses by different physicians.

Strains and sprains

If the ankle is twisted suddenly the ligaments are overstretched and become swollen and very painful. In other words we have a sprained ankle. In the damaged ligament there may be bleeding and torn fibres. There is some inflammation which helps to repair the injury but also adds to the swelling. That ligament may occasionally be permanently damaged, or overstretched so that the support for the ankle is weak and the ankle can easily be injured again.

The same sort of problem may affect the back. A sudden movement of the spine may overstretch and strain the ligaments around the vertebral column in just the same way as at the ankle. The damaged ligaments are painful and yet the ranges of movements of the back are normal or even increased. The continued movement leads to further ligament strains.

Those double-jointed people described earlier may meet the same sort of problem. With their excessive flexibility they may stress the spine to such extremes that damage to a ligament takes place.

Ligaments can be strained in another way. To take a simple example, if one rests in a chair with the feet up on a stool, aching and stiffness may develop in the back of the knee. This is due to stretching of the ligaments behind the knee joint. Similarly, if one sits or stands in a poor posture then the various ligaments connecting the vertebrae may be over-stretched and this will lead to an aching pain felt in the back. Most of us experience this if we sit for a long time in a soft armchair without any back support. When we get up and move about the aching and stiffness gradually disappear.

In people with strained ligaments the spine usually retains a good range of movement—if anything, greater than normal. Carefully feeling the back may show an area of tenderness, particularly if a ligament near the surface is damaged. Pressure at this point may reproduce the symptoms.

Following damage to the ligament there is a repair process in which fibrous tissue is formed. This is a scar that stiffens the ligament so that in the end movements become more limited than before the accident. An area of fibrous stiffening is called an adhesion and may be painful because it is stretched during relatively normal movements. The persistent stiffness seen in the back after injury is due to adhesions around the joints of the spine. Sometimes adhesions form around nerve roots so that back movements pull on the nerves and produce pain in the back and lower limbs. The most severe examples of adhesions can occur in those patients who have worn a lumbo-sacral corset for a long time after a back injury. They have kept their spines very still and avoided movements and the end-result is this severe stiffness. Any attempt at movement produces severe pain because of stretching of the adhesions. I call this condition a 'stuck back'. In many cases it is a further example of the chronic inflammation and scar tissue formation which is described in detail in Chapter 8.

Fibrositis and fibromyalgia

Fibrositis is a common complaint, and yet no one really understands what it is. The term 'fibrositis' refers to pains felt in localized areas across the shoulders or in the back. There are very tender and painful spots or nodules in the muscles and the symptoms become much worse with any exercise. Careful feeling sometimes indicates that the muscle in that area is contracting continuously or, in other words, in spasm. The reason why this happens is not clear but the result is that the blood supply in that area is poor and the waste materials formed during normal muscle contraction are not carried away. This may contribute to the pain. Usually these painful areas will respond to a local injection of a pain-relieving drug (Chapter 7).

The fibromyalgia syndrome is an unpleasant condition in which fibrositic nodules continually recur particularly around the back of the shoulders and across the low back but often also in the legs. The patients suffer aching and stiffness particularly across the neck and back but sometimes everywhere. An injection may relieve an individual episode of pain but commonly it will recur either at that site or elsewhere within a short period of time. The cause of the fibromyalgia syndrome is not known but it is usually associated with a very poor sleep pattern. Patients often find that they cannot get a good night's sleep. They toss and turn and do not feel refreshed when they get up in the morning. At that time they feel very stiff and their symptoms are at their worst. I think it is very much like an overnight aircraft flight. One sleeps poorly on the plane and gets out at the other end feeling aching and stiff. Research does suggest that poor sleeping is important. It is possible to measure the electrical activity of the brain and determine exactly how deeply one is sleeping. Healthy volunteers underwent tests in which their brain electrical activities were measured. Everytime they fell into a deep sleep they were gently stimulated not to wake up but simply to disturb their sleep. In the mornings they had aching and stiffness problems exactly like the fibromyalgia patients. This information has been helpful in treating their condition. Not only are pain-relieving injections used but measures to improve the quality of sleep, exercises and general attention to physical fitness seem to be very helpful.

Some patients develop localized tender points at the sites of attachments of ligaments to the back. These areas are known as entheses and some people are prone to developing pain in these sites all over the body. It may be around the elbows, shoulders, knees, hips, back, and elswhere. Generally no cause for this condition can be found but in a small proportion of patients it is related to ankylosing spondylitis (Chapter 10).

Sacro-iliac pain

The pain may be felt in one of the two sacro-iliac joints. These joints connect the sacrum or tail bone to the rest of the pelvis and are based low down in the back with one on each side. They are complicated, irregular joints that usually only allow a limited amount of movement. Inflammation occurs in the sacro-iliac joints in ankylosing spondylitis. However, mechanical damage commonly causes pain in these joints, as may pregnancy. In the female pelvis it is normal for the various ligaments to become much looser at about the time of childbirth so that the pelvis can enlarge and the baby be delivered without damage. During the later stages of pregnancy backache is common and this is partly due to the looseness of the various ligaments allowing the pelvic joints to widen combined with the extra strain on the back produced by the weight of the pregnant womb. Once childbirth is completed the ligaments gradually return to their normal condition and the looseness of the sacro-iliac and other joints disappears. In some women, however, the joints may not return to exactly their previous fit and the ligaments may remain overstretched. These sacro-iliac joints can be very painful. The pain is felt in the low back in one or other sacro-iliac joint and is made worse by bending and twisting movements. Mothers have to do a lot of bending, particularly when looking after a new-born child, and consequently often have backache and tenderness in the area of these joints.

Other problems

There are many other types of backache that do not fit readily into these groups. The nature of the symptoms and the examination findings will indicate no serious illness but suggest that there is some form of mechanical problem. It is valuable to be able to reassure the patient that there is nothing seriously amiss but at the same time we must acknowledge that the current state of affairs is still unsatisfactory. With the greater insight into non-specific back pain that we have today, and by using newer diagnostic methods, we are gradually learning to identify the underlying problems. There have been real advances but there is still a long way to go.

5

Physical methods of treatment

Introduction

Back pain can develop for so many different reasons that it is no small wonder that there is such a wide variety of forms of treatment. The problems of defining the precise cause of the pain are reflected in the often difficult decisions about the best types of treatment. What is suitable for one back sufferer may be quite useless for another. Some people appear to respond rapidly and effectively to one type of treatment whereas others with superficially similar problems fail to obtain any benefit. As we get better at establishing the precise causes of the back pain we become able to offer more definite advice and help. However, in many cases the types of treatment used depend predominantly on the severity and nature of the symptoms, rather than being specifically directed at the underlying problem. Clearly the long-term future lies in acquiring a better understanding of the spine and its problems.

This chapter describes the physical treatment of patients with the various mechanical types of back pain. The control of pain, as opposed to treatment of the back, is described in Chapter 6, and injections and operations in Chapter 7. The spinal problems associated with other disorders such as ankylosing spondylitis, Paget's disease, tumours, and so on are considered separately under their appropriate headings.

Many patients with back problems suffer from acute episodes of pain and disability with little problem in between. It is usually relatively straightforward to deal with these acute attacks but continuous or recurrent problems can be much more difficult.

Bed rest

For the patient with very severe low back pain, a spell of complete rest in bed will usually clear the symptoms rapidly.

In the past, patients were told to rest until the pain got better. Sometimes this could take several weeks and thereafter there would be a gradual process of recovery. Recent research now tells us that this was the wrong advice. A short period of rest is very helpful but a longer period of bed rest can actually prolong the duration of the pain and delay the process of recovery. We now believe that the period of bed rest should only be for a couple of days and thereafter the patient should gradually return to normal physical activity. Careful measurements suggest that pain will go away more quickly and the patient return to work more rapidly with this short period of bed rest compared with the prolonged periods previously recommended.

So the general advice for someone with acute pain and stiffness is to go to bed lying flat, with one pillow for just two days. I allow my patients up to wash and to go to the toilet because the strain on the back is much less if one gets up briefly than trying to perch precariously on a bed pan or struggling to wash while lying flat. After this short period the patient should gradually start to get up, sit out, and move around but taking care to protect the back as described later in this chapter.

Beds

Not all beds are the same. Following a night in a poor bed many of us will wake in the morning with aching and stiffness in the back. This problem is far worse for the back pain sufferer and if put to bed it is essential that the bed conditions are right. The big problem is that many beds are soft and sag under the weight of the body (Fig. 13). The softness of the bed is often equated with quality but this is not so. A good bed will have a soft surface which is resilient and does not sag. If the bed is too soft the weight of the body will make the bed give, so that the spine lies in a curved position. Lying on one's side makes the back curve sideways and lying on one's back makes it bend forward. Both these positions can make the symptoms much worse.

How can one obtain the ideal bed, and what should one do if suddenly confronted with the need to provide bed rest for the back sufferer? The simplest answer is to place a board under the mattress and on top of the base of the bed. This board will support the mattress and prevent sagging without making the bed uncomfortable. The board should be the full length of the bed and at least as wide

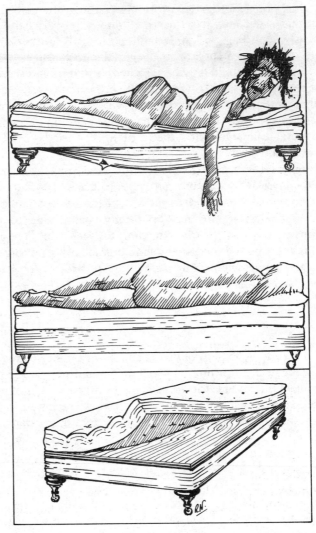

Fig. 13 Beds. *Upper*: The sag in a poor bed. *Centre*: The support from a properly sprung bed. *Lower*: A board under the mattress

as the patient. It should be rigid enough not to bend under the body weight. Three-quarter-inch or 2 cm blockboard seems a very good material for this purpose. Smaller boards are available and also folding boards that may be taken by back sufferers with them if they have to sleep away from home. Although helpful, these folding boards cost a lot more and are not quite as rigid as the type of board first described. For people who sleep in a double bed it is often a good idea for the board to be placed under both partners. Sleeping with a board is remarkably comfortable and even the non-sufferer may be pleasantly surprised once he has tried it. Because double beds are so large, two separate boards side by side underneath the mattress may be better.

An alternative way of providing support to the back during the night is to place the mattress directly on the floor. It can be a bit draughty but as far as the back is concerned it does just as well. The hardness of the surface and the cold do not seem to worry them. For most back sufferers, however, this is not necessary.

The ideal solution may be to buy a bed which will give appropriate support. This is where the quality of the bed comes in. A cheap bed contains few springs which are widely spaced so that it readily sags under a load. This can usually be recognized simply by sitting on the edge of the bed when the 'give' is all too obvious. In better-quality products there are many more springs which are set closer together. There is much firmer and smoother support, preventing sagging. Unfortunately quality has its price and the cost of the better beds can be much higher than that of the cheaper products. Any reputable shop selling beds will provide information about the firmness of their products and about their construction.

'Orthopaedic' beds are widely advertised as being suitable for the back pain patient. In this context the word 'orthopaedic' means that the bed is particularly firm. The term 'ortho' means straight and 'paedic' refers to children so that the original use of the word orthopaedic referred to the type of surgeon who corrected the deformities of crippled children. It then came to refer to surgeons who dealt with all disorders of the bones and joints but is not at all clear why this adjective should be attached to the description of a bed when no surgery is involved. The adjective orthopaedic is often used to justify an enormous increase in the cost of the bed compared with other similar products which are obtainable at much more reasonable prices.

When buying a bed it is important to choose one that is appropriate and comfortable for the person who will use it. Lie on the bed in the shop for a few minutes and see that it feels comfortable and that there is no sagging. However, a bed that is too firm and too hard can be uncomfortable. There is no better way than trying it out for oneself. There is no general rule about which bed is best. A large, heavy person may need a different type of bed from a small, light person. In some cases one person in a couple needs a firm bed but the other prefers a relatively soft bed, and there are combination beds that may be zipped together to give this type of arrangement.

The position in bed is all important for the acute back pain patient. The aim is to place the spine in the best position to avoid stretching nerves, ligaments, and other structures in the back. This is best achieved by lying flat in bed, with only one pillow but with the hips slightly flexed and the lower legs resting on a pillow. In this the hollowing in the small of the back is straightened out and pressure on the damaged tissue, and stretching of the nerves and ligaments minimized. The precise arrangements often vary for any individual. If a position is comfortable and relieves the pain then it is likely that this is suitable for allowing healing of the damaged tissues.

The patient with severe back pain should rest in bed. However, this description of beds and sleeping arrangements applies to any back sufferer. Many patients with backache have some of the worst symptoms at night or first thing in the morning. Lying flat with a firm bed will usually make an enormous difference to these problems.

This advice about beds applies not only to people with back pain but may be used as a guide for anybody seeking to purchase a bed. Even people without backache will find that a firm bed with proper support is much more comfortable than one that sags too readily. Calculations show that the average person spends 23 years of his life in bed. It must be worthwhile getting one that is comfortable. In other countries people are accustomed to different types of beds. In the United States they are usually much firmer than in Britain and American visitors often complain of discomfort and back problems due to the soft beds when visiting the UK.

Why does bed rest help?

Very severe attacks of back pain and sciatica are usually due to damage in the spine and often a burst intervertebral disc. There is not only the mechanical problem produced by the injury but also some inflammation of the damaged tissues. The inflamed tissues are swollen and produce pain. Every time the back moves these swollen tissues are rubbed, producing more pain and more inflammation. In this way keeping active never allows the injured part of the body to heal. A short period of complete bed rest lets the inflammation settle and hastens the process of healing. Again, a rather crude comparison can be drawn with a boil. If it is continually rubbed it will take a long time to get better but left alone it will clear up rapidly.

Curvature of the spine stretches the nerves and the ligaments. When the spine is straight there is the least strain on them. This is why it is important to avoid sagging.

As the pain clears up the patient gradually starts moving again. At first things should be taken very cautiously but within a week or two the patient should be able to get back to reasonable activity. However, he must always be careful to avoid stressing his back. Advice on posture and the correct ways to bend and lift will be given later.

The recovery period

We are dealing with back pain due to mechanical damage, and clearly any undue strain of the back can make this worse. It is very important to make sure that no undue stress arises, particularly during the healing phase after an acute attack of pain. It is only too easy to damage the back again and lose the benefit from a boring period of bed rest. Getting out of bed should be done gradually and carefully, using the arms to push oneself up sideways and avoiding bending the back as much as possible. When standing one should not perform sudden movements, particularly if they involve bending and twisting. Any movement that produces pain is bad and should be avoided. When first getting up it may be helpful to hold on to a rail or some other object in order to get support.

Avoid lifting altogether if possible. If it is really necessary the load must not be too heavy and it is better to divide it into two or more parts rather than lift a single heavy object. Lifts from the floor should always be done by bending at the knees with one foot behind and the other at the side of the object keeping the spine straight rather than flexing forwards. This is described in detail in Chapter 9.

When lifting an object, take up the strain gradually rather than suddenly. A sudden jolt to the back may be enough to cause another attack of back pain. When carrying any weight it should be held as close to the body as possible. This is because holding it further away produces a much greater stress on the spine than when it is held close. Above all do not carry any object that is too heavy.

When sitting down the type of chair is all-important. Chairs for back sufferers, or indeed for any of us, are dealt with in detail in Chapter 9. Here suffice it so say that the chair must be of the right height and provide support in the small of the back. Low armchairs with soft padding might superficially look comfortable but they can make the back problem much worse. An upright chair with a built-in lumbar support or a small pillow placed in the hollow of the back is better and very much more comfortable.

Instruction on the care of the back is all important. If you know how to protect the back it is relatively easy to avoid stressful situations and to prevent recurrence of the problem. This process of instruction has been carried to an extreme in Sweden where they have now developed 'back schools'. The whole treatment programme revolves around teaching the back sufferer about the structure of his back, what may go wrong, and how to protect it against further damage. There are a series of class lessons and at the end of the course the patient takes an examination which will not only tell whether he has understood all that has gone on, but also act as a revision exercise, going over much of the material covered in the course. The Swedish doctors and physiotherapists who run the back school feel that the end-results are as good as those obtained using other types of treatment. Their work looks promising and back schools are now developing in Centres in Britain, the rest of Europe, North America, and elsewhere. Having an understanding of the problem can only help—after all that is the reason why this book has been written.

Traction

It is a constant source of amazement to me that traction as a treatment for back pain has been used for many centuries and persists in principle relatively unchanged to this day. Moreover, despite the frequency with which it is practised, we do not know how traction works, and indeed there is still doubt about whether it works at all.

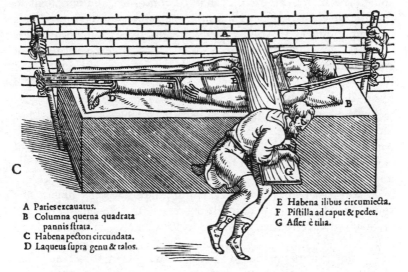

A Paries excauatus.
B Columna querna quadrata
    pannis strata.
C Habena pectori circundata.
D Laqueus supra genu & talos.

E Habena ilibus circumiecta.
F Pistilla ad caput & pedes.
G Asser è tilia.

Fig. 14 Traction combined with pressure on the spine as recommended by Hippocrates. By courtesy of the Wellcome Trustees

Hippocrates was a physician in ancient Greece and his writings are still relevant to many medical problems today. He treated back pain by traction in which the patient lay prone on a board known as a scamnum. Ropes were tied to the upper and lower parts of the body and a winch tightened, so stretching the spine. This treatment was often accompanied by some form of manipulation. Sometimes the manipulator walked barefoot over the stretched spine. Barefoot manipulation, often by female manipulators, is still practised today and is said by some to be remarkably relaxing, particularly if performed under appropriate circumstances!

Another technique used in ancient Greece was to hang the poor back sufferer upside-down by his ankles from an upright ladder. The ladder was then shaken vigorously and the pain was said to get better. Of course if the pain got worse there was little the patient could do about it in such extenuating circumstances. This has its counterpart in some forms of modern treatment. The patient may

lie on a special rotating frame with the feet firmly held in a pair of
'gravity boots'. The frame then rotates slowly so that the patient
may come to lie upside down suspended from the feet and the
weight of the body produces traction or stretching forces on the
spine. The amount of rotation may be controlled by the patient so
that the weight experienced should not be increased too much. This
technique utilizes the body's own weight and is known as auto-
traction. Although this may appear to be an exciting form of
treatment we have yet to learn whether it is really of value. There
have been patients whose feet have come out of their boots when
upside down and fallen on their heads with dire consequences!

Another related technique practised by some people is a form of
'do-it-yourself' traction. The subject stands against a door with his
hands hooked over the upper edge and then gradually relaxes and
bends the knees until the feet are lifted off the floor. It is all-
important to do this slowly and carefully as otherwise it not only
makes the back pain worse, but also pulls the door off its hinges. The
spine should be twisted carefully from side to side and the weight
gradually transferred back to the feet as soon as the hands begin to
tire.

Traction is sometimes used for people with acute back pain when
confined to bed. Bandages are tied around each leg and a rope is
bound into each bandage. The two ropes from each leg run over
pulleys positioned at the foot of the bed and weights of a few
pounds are attached to each. In order to stop the traction pulling the
subject down the bed, the foot of the bed is raised a few inches so
that the body will counterbalance the weights. The stretching force
applied is very mild as it is kept on for long periods. As such it is
doubtful whether such force actually does anything to the spine.
More likely it is a very effective means of making sure the subject
rests properly as it is not possible to get out of bed without undoing
the traction.

With intermittent traction, much more powerful forces are
applied. This is performed under the close supervision of a
physiotherapist to make sure no damage is done. The subject is
strapped with a harness around the lower chest and pelvis and lies
on a special traction couch. The two halves of the body are pulled
apart so that the low back is stretched with forces of up to 30–60 kg
(70–130 lb) (Plate 6). The precise arrangement varies with the back
problem, the type of couch, and the physiotherapist giving the

treatment. The couch is positioned so that the subject is comfortable and the stretching is arranged so as to avoid making the symptoms worse. The pull may be either continuous for several minutes or gentle repetitive rhythmic pulses of stretching and relaxing. Speculation has it that rhythmic traction improves the circulation to the spine.

It is not at all clear what traction does to the back and how it may relieve back pain. The original idea was that the tiny facet joints in the back of the spine had become displaced and that pulling on the spine would bring them back into alignment. However, examination of the spine produces no evidence to support this. Another theory was that stretching the spine would suck the 'slipped disc' back into its original place in a similar fashion to the way we can suck toothpaste back into a half empty tube by stretching the tube. However, we now know that discs do not slip but burst and it is difficult to see how traction on the spine could suck a burst disc back again. It could be that pulling on muscles that have contracted in spasm may gradually make them relax and so relieve the pain.

It is difficult to assess the value of traction as it is commonly combined with other forms of treatment. Most patients with acute back pain and sciatica confined to bed will get better within a few days or a couple of weeks. It is difficult to say whether traction actually hastens this process or simply makes the bed-rest more effective. When given on an intermittent basis it is often combined with heat, exercises, or manipulation. Most patients slowly improve after a short period of regular treatment. In a careful study conducted at St Thomas' Hospital in London, patients were given intermittent traction either with the full force for 30 minutes per day, five days per week for three weeks, or extremely light traction given in a similar fashion. Those receiving the full force did slightly better than those receiving only minimal traction but analysis of the statistics did not indicate that the extra improvement was of real significance. So it remains an open question whether traction either by itself or in combination with other forms of treatment is of real value.

Heat and cold

We all know how comforting warmth can be for backache. A warm bath or a hot water bottle can be remarkably relaxing. Those prone to backache often wear thermal underwear such as angora wool vests. In many countries the national dress seems to reflect this and the wide woollen cummerbunds found in many peasant costumes could well have developed on this basis. In Victorian Britain, Doll's flannel was traditionally worn and seems to have had the same purpose.

On the other hand, draughts are notorious for producing backache. It is not at all clear why this should be. One theory is that exposure to cold makes blood vessels contract, reducing the blood supply to the tissues in and around the spine and causing pain. Another suggestion is simply that lying in a draught often means that one is keeping still in an uncomfortable position for a long period. Either or both of these may be true. All we know is that in some unknown way lying in a chill can exacerbate back pain.

This sort of experience led to the use of heat to relieve backache. The simpler method is to apply a hot water bottle or expose the back to a radiant fire. Many people do this for themselves and they must always be extremely careful not to overdo things and burn their back. It is often easy to see that patients have been applying radiant heat to the back as it produces a curious and persistent mottling of the skin which can last for a long time after stopping the treatment.

Heat is frequently used by physiotherapists as part of a programme for back pain. They do not believe that the heat alters the underlying problem or makes any difference to the long-term outcome. However, it is effective at relieving the symptoms at the time it is given and they use it as an adjunct to other types of treatment. Heat is given to the stiff and painful back as a preliminary to exercise or manipulation.

Heat can be applied directly to the back using electric heating pads. This heats the skin but is not very effective at heating the deeper tissues. Both infra-red and short-wave diathermy are able to penetrate the skin and therefore seem more effective. Infra-red is a form of heat radiation similar to light waves but of a wavelength beyond the extremes of the visual spectrum. All hot objects radiate infra-red waves but some materials are much more effective radiators than others. Radiant heat lamps are very efficient and the infra-red radiation is applied to the back in a careful fashion and a measured amount of heat given. The short-wave diathermy machine is very different. Electric currents circulate in a special coil placed over the back. They induce electric currents beneath the surface of the skin and generate heat within the body tisses. The short-wave diathermy apparatus is extremely expensive. There is now real doubt about whether it has any advantage over simpler methods of applying heat. In some recent studies in which the temperature was actually measured beneath the surface of the skin, it was found that the temperature rise is very much less than previously thought. Moreover, there are special problems with short-wave diathermy as it can induce very strong currents if there are any metallic objects beneath the coil of the machines. Short-wave is now used much less frequently than it was a few years ago.

Massage

Massage, or the rhythmical application of pressure by the hands, can be remarkably comforting for people with acutely painful backs. A skilled masseuse can relax tight, knotted muscles and dissipate much of the pain. Although such treatment sounds remarkably pleasant and comforting, unfortunately in the long run it does not actually alter the course of the back pain. It does nothing to the underlying problem, but merely alleviates the symptoms for the time that it is given. Massage may work by altering the perception of pain rather than by improving the damaged tissues. This will be described in Chapter 6.

Massage seems more helpful for people with acutely strained backs than those with long-standing chronic back problems. It is sometimes given in combination with other types of treatment making manipulation and other procedures less painful. This type of treatment is sometimes used for sportsmen with a minor injury when skilled massage combined with heat and exercises may get them back to full activity more quickly.

It therefore seems that massage has a minor but nevertheless helpful part to play in treating some back problems. It is unfortunate that the technique has become synonymous in the popular press with various types of sexual activity and the masseuse with a therapist of a not strictly medical kind. This has led to loss of the skills possessed by practioners of this technique. Although they seem of limited value nevertheless they can be helpful under appropriate circumstances.

Various types of liniments are sometimes used. They are slightly irritant ointments rubbed into the skin over the painful part. Reddening of the skin results partly due to the chemicals within the liniment but also due to the actual rubbing itself and indeed this is another form of massage. The relief of pain seems to be due to a combination of both these factors. Recently, some of the pain-relieving anti-inflammatory medicine such as ibuprofen (Brufen), diclofenac (Voltarol), piroxicam (Feldene), tenoxican (Traxam), and others have become available as creams or gels. They may be rubbed into the painful area. Some of the liniment is absorbed through the skin and may ease the pain.

Exercises

At first sight exercises seem the obvious way to cure the stiff and painful back. Stiffness should improve and painful joints and ligaments can be eased back into normal use. The keep-fit experts extoll the virtues of exercises and mobility in the belief that physical fitness can prevent and cure most ills. However, what may seem obvious is not necessarily true. Even the fittest athletes may be struck down by acute attacks of back pain and those lazy members of society who avoid virtually all forms of physical activity may escape without any significant back problems.

Do regular exercises prevent back pain?

This question is not as easy to answer as it seems because, although on the whole fit people get fewer back problems than those who do not take regular exercise, it may simply be that those with backache are not as good at sport or keep-fit classes and therefore turn their attentions elsewhere. The inference to be drawn is not that performing athletics prevents the development of back pain but that people with backache do not become great athletes. Future research should help to solve this conundrum.

What about the value of exercises for a person who has had, or who is recovering from an episode of back pain? Is exercise good or can it harm the back? What sorts of exercises are suitable and how should they be done?

There are various types of exercise programmes and what is effective depends very much on the nature of the individual problem. In recent years we have learned an enormous amount about the importance of exercise and there has been a dramatic revolution in our approach to this aspect of treatment. In particular in the old days we believed in prolonged periods of rest and immobilizing the back in a spinal corset. Today the emphasis has changed. We now believe the spine is meant to move and exercising the back is helpful. Prolonged periods of inactivity should be avoided.

If the pain is very severe perhaps with sciatica in the leg and there is a lot of spasm of the back muscles, forced movements of the back can make the problem much worse. If a particular movement produces severe pain then that exercise is best avoided. On the other hand, even if some exercises may be a bit painful, as long as they do not produce severe pain then they help. We now advise intensive exercise rehabilitation programmes and recent research has shown that carefully graded but determined exercise can transform the rehabilitation process. Exercises may be painful but they should not damage and the watchword in many physiotherapy departments is now 'hurt does not mean harm'. Indeed, if no pain is felt it suggests that the exercise is inadequate and the second guiding rule may be 'no pain, no gain'.

Why does exercise help? There are several different reasons. The joints in the back may be stiff due to adhesions and moving them can gradually restore them to their normal range. The muscles may become weak; exercise can improve their strength so that less strain is carried by the bones and joints. We now know that the blood circulation around the nerves is affected in many back pain problems. Exercise will improve the circulation within the spine much as exercise is used to improve the circulation in heart blood vessels in patients with angina or heart attacks. Many back sufferers lack confidence and are frightened to use their backs. An exercise programme will teach them that they can use their backs and will help them to return to normal activity.

Types of exercises

In mobilizing exercises, the principal aim is to improve the movements of the back by bending the spine in all directions in an effort to overcome the stiffness in the various joints. These exercises are practised by sportsmen and women and clearly are of great importance in keeping fit. However the back pain sufferer has a totally different problem and very vigorous exercises of this sort do more harm than good. Very forceful extreme movements can further damage the back and these types of exercises should only be undertaken under careful professional supervision.

There are only two problems for which these mobilizing exercises are right. The first is a quite different condition, namely ankylosing spondylitis, which will be described in Chapter 10. The second is for people who have had an attack of back pain and then have worn a corset for a very long time thereafter. If the spine is not allowed to move properly for such a long period, adhesions may develop between the joints so that the spine becomes extremely stiff and all movements very painful. At this stage movements in all directions are severely limited and any attempt at bending stretches the adhesions and produces pain. I call this a 'stuck back' and I think it is as much due to the past treatment as to the original back injury. This problem is described in more detail in Chapter 8. For certain such patients I believe that mobilizing exercises can be very helpful. They stretch the adhesion and gradually improve the movements of the back. Of course, as the back has been stuck for such a long time mobilization can be a very painful process and pain-relieving tablets are necessary. If the patient persists with the exercises it may be possible to get the back almost to normal. It is important that this treatment is carefully supervised to make sure no harm is being done.

In flexion exercises the emphasis is on forward bending. Not only are these perfomed standing upright, as previously described, but also lying flat on the ground with the hands above the head and then forcibly sitting up and bending forwards to touch the toes with the legs outstretched. These exercises produce very high stresses in the spine and enormous pressures in the intervertebral discs. Although they may be suitable for athletes who aim to keep themselves in the peak of condition, generally they are not right for the back sufferer. The bending movements can squeeze the discs and stretch the ligaments. A burst disc that has healed can easily burst again under these circumstances. Back sufferers should not perform these forcible flexion exercises.

Similar doubts arise about extension exercises, in which the subject stands upright and forcibly arches backwards. The bones in the back of the spine normally carry an excessive proportion of the load compared with other parts of the vertebral column. Arching backwards increases this and can add to damage in the tiny facet joints in the back of the spine. Studies comparing these extension exercises with other types of treatment have shown that they do not help, and for some people they may make things worse.

The types of exercises that are of real value are known as 'isometric' exercises. These are aimed at building up the muscles of the back and also of the wall of the abdomen or tummy. Strengthening the spine muscles provides much better control of back movements, and enables the patient to lift and perform other activities with less stress on the bones. Improvement of the power of the muscles in the abdomen will increase the pressure that can be produced in the abdomen and therefore will relieve the back of a greater proportion of its load. Isometric exercises will produce these benefits without stressing the spine itself and therefore are very helpful.

The word 'isometric' comes from 'iso' which means equal and 'metric' which refers to length. Isometric contraction of a muscle means that the muscles contract without altering their length. Pulling on a rigid object is an example of an isometric contraction. If the object moves then the contraction is no longer isometric. The principle of isometric exercise is applied to the spine by making various muscles contract but with only limited movements of the back itself (Plate 7).

The muscles of the abdomen can be strengthened by lying flat on the floor, pointing the toes, and raising the head to look at them. Another method is to lie flat, keep the legs straight and raise them just above the ground, hold them for a few seconds and then lower them slowly to the floor. These are very effective exercises for the abdominal muscles and do not stress the spine at all. The back muscles can also be strengthened by lying prone or face downwards with the arms by the sides and then lifting first the head and shoulders and then the legs alternately. Each position should be held for a few seconds and then relaxed. Each movement is performed half a dozen times. It is only necessary to lift the head and shoulders and the legs off the ground and the back should not be arched excessively. If pain is produced the exercise should be done more gently. However, all exercises are tailored for the individual and his problem, and the physician and physiotherapist will advise on what is appropriate.

In general, exercise treatment is directed at strengthening muscles rather than improving the movements. It is only too easy to make the back worse and any exercise or movement that produces pain should be avoided.

Manipulation

Of all the problems associated with back pain it is the question of manipulation that gives rise to the greatest controversy. A wide variety of different manipulative techniques is practised both by doctors and lay practitioners. The different methods are taught in different schools often with no agreement as to when manipulation is indicated, what is being treated, how the manipulation should be done, what actually happens during the manipulation, or the short- and long-term results of treatment. Moreover, personal views are often expressed vehemently but without any factual basis.

We have all heard of patients severely disabled by back pain who obtained immediate relief following a manipulation. Nevertheless the overall value of these procedures remains in doubt. Some studies have been performed to determine whether manipulation works. Despite these investigations a solid case in favour of manipulation remains unproven. My own studies of these techniques will be described. A recent working group convened by the Medical Research Council to investigate the whole back problem has pointed the need for further research.

The mechanical basis for the majority of back problems suggests the possibility of a mechanical solution. If, as osteopaths suggest, there is a spinal 'lesion' or 'derangement' which consists of slightly dislocated or subluxed joint or some loss of mobility, then a manipulation may put things right. But it is not as easy as that. Many back problems arise from a burst of the disc. No amount of manipulation can repair a burst. A damaged ligament cannot be repaired by manipulation. So the controversy persists, although to the patient what matters is whether the technique works rather than why or how it is done.

The origins of manipulation

The word 'manipulate' when applied to the spine refers specifically to manual pressure on the back in an attempt to remedy defects. In biblical times physicians believed that back pain could arise because the bones were out of alignment and that manipulation could line them up again. The Greek physician Galen described methods of combining pressure on the spine with traction techniques in an effort to restore alignment. Nevertheless manipulation did not find favour with the medical profession in succeeding centuries and was largely ignored until quite recently.

Until about a century ago medicine and surgery were different professions. The physician believed in the prescription of elegant mixtures of medicines which commonly had little or no therapeutic action, but were usually impressively coloured and unpleasant to take. The surgeon was there to operate and performed such procedures as amputations, opening of the abdomen for various types of stones, and stitching wounds. The patient with a strained joint would often go to the bone-setter who would try to put things right by giving the joint a wrench or a twist. The physicians and surgeons of the day looked down on bone-setting as a crude, unprofessional, working-class type of treatment and not to be considered in the sophisticated society in which they mixed. Nevertheless some bone-setters developed reputations of being able to treat bad backs and enquiring minds began to examine the value of these procedures.

Bone-setting was a very crude form of manipulation. Little attempt was made to identify what had gone wrong and why. Rather all patients received the same type of treatment, for better or worse. The bone-setters were practical people, not theorists, and did not worry too much about whether they actually did what they thought they were doing but whether they got good results. They believed they could realign displaced joints by breaking down the adhesions, holding them out of alignment, and then reducing them back into the appropriate position with a satisfying 'plop'.

Perhaps the most famous bone-setter was Herbert Barker who practised in Manchester and London in the early part of the twentieth century. His work was condemned by the medical profession and his case was made worse by being sued by a youth whose tuberculous leg he had treated and which later was amputated. Nevertheless his reputation grew. He developed a reputation for treating back pain for which eventually he was knighted. Whether his results would stand up to critical modern analysis will never be known.

Osteopathy

The bone-setters were practical men who practised their art according to rules which neglected whys and wherefores and only sought results. Osteopathy, on the other hand, grew up with a theoretical basis. Although osteopathic techniques may well be helpful, many of the original ideas were extremely controversial and subsequently have been discarded.

The founder of osteopathy, Andrew Taylor Still, was an American physician in the nineteenth century. He is not to be confused with George Frederick Still of the Hospital for Sick Children, Great Ormond Street in London, who first described arthritis in children. A. T. Still believed that the spinal cord and the nerves, particularly in the neck, controlled the blood flow in the limbs and elsewhere. Disorders of the spine, such as a strain or a partial dislocation that he called a 'Subluxation', could disturb the blood flow and produce various types of symptoms. By manipulating the neck he believed it possible to improve the blood flow and cure all sorts of symptoms and diseases. Osteopaths believed in the osteopathic 'lesion'—disorder of the intervertebral joints which could produce not only pain in that area but also many other problems including heart and lung disease and various abdominal upsets. The extravagance of the osteopaths' claims were unacceptable to the medical profession and led the whole subject into disrepute.

Today most osteopaths believe firmly that their form of treatment may help various types of spinal disorder and the pain that is produced by pressure on nerves and other structures, but that the excessive claims of past years are best forgotten.

The osteopath will examine the spine for what he calls a 'lesion' or derangement. Carefully feeling this area reveals some loss of the normal mobility in an intervertebral joint. We do not know the pathological basis for this osteopathic lesion—if indeed there is one. Many different things can go wrong in the spine and in life it is often difficult if not impossible to prove what has happened to produce the impaired mobility about which the osteopaths speak. The osteopaths themselves are in doubt and suggest a malalignment of the vertebrae, adhesions between the joints in mobile segments, and other explanations.

Osteopaths carry the technique of palpation to a fine art and use a variety of terms to describe the changes in the various spinal segments. These findings are entirely subjective and it is very doubtful whether they would stand up to comparison by two different experts examining the same patient.

Once the area believed responsible for the problem is identified the osteopath will manipulate the spine. When patients are seen repeatedly the preliminary examination is always performed first so that the manipulative technique can be modified according to the patient's progress.

The treatment involves relaxing the muscles around the affected part by careful stretching and manipulation, moving the affected joints carefully and repeatedly until free, and following this with a 'high-velocity thrust' using lever techniques on the pelvis and other parts of the body. The patient is usually positioned on his side and with a twist to the trunk so that other joints in the back are believed to be locked and only those that require treatment are free. The 'thrust' may sometimes produce a tearing noise and a click. It is uncertain what produces these sounds. Some osteopaths think that they represent the tearing of adhesions between joints and therefore regard them as a good thing. In fact we do not know what is happening and there does seem some potential risk if unknown tissues are being damaged internally.

Of course what counts in the end is whether the treatment works, and it is all too easy to adopt a rough and ready approach and say that if any practitioner can make the back better then he should get on with it. While this is true the statement does contain a big 'if'. Although many backs do improve after an osteopathic manipulation it remains to be proven that the treatment itself was responsible for the improvement and that it has made any long-term difference. What is certain is that any manipulative therapy should only be given by someone who is properly trained. Although robust, the spine is a very complicated structure containing many delicate nerves and tiny blood vessels. Unskilled or wrong treatment can do a lot of harm.

Does osteopathy work? If it can be proven helpful then all else will be forgiven. The techniques would be adopted by the medical profession and particularly by those concerned with treating pain. Before too long the osteopaths might find themselves out of business.

Attacks of back pain do not normally persist indefinitely but come and go with acute episodes that may last a few hours, days, or weeks, but will almost always partially or totally clear up until the next bout develops. If treatment is given during an acute attack the chances are that the attack will get better anyway and it is uncertain whether the treatment itself was responsible for the improvement. We know that the vast majority of patients who suddenly develop back pain get better within a few days. On the other hand, if the back pain has been present for weeks or months the outlook is not nearly as good. This means that it is the patients with the recent history of back pain who will do best even if untreated but it is precisely this group which has been identified by the osteopath as likely to benefit from his manipulations. How do we know that the high rate of recovery in these patients is due to his treatment rather than the natural recovery rate?

Anecdotal stories of people with persistent back problems who get better immediately after osteopathic manipulation are quite common but equally I have known patients who have described similar improvement after forms of treatment which could not possibly be of any value. Nevertheless some patients do get better and the question must still be asked whether osteopathic manipulation does have some immediate benefit.

In a previous edition of this book I complained that the techniques of osteopathic manipulation have never been submitted to the types of scientific enqury and testing that are routine for all other branches of medicine. Since then the first proper trial of osteopathy has been performed. It was conducted by an osteopath working with doctors in Guy's Hospital in London. Patients who developed back pain were seen by an osteopath who was allowed to choose those whom he thought most likely to benefit from manipulation. They were then randomly divided into three groups. One group received manipulation by the osteopath, another received deep heat treatment, and the third the application of the same deep heat machine but with the current turned down so low as to be totally ineffective. After the course of treatment the patients were examined by a physician who did not know what form of treatment had been given so that he could report on the patients progress without being biased. The results showed that immediately after the treatment 59 per cent were improved after the deep heat, 67 per cent after deep heat with the machine turned down, but only 62 per cent after osteopathic manipulation. Likewise the investigators analysed the numbers who were unable to fulfil their normal activities at home and at work. All three groups showed improvements but these were only significant in those receiving deep heat and the deep heat machine turned down and not in those who were manipulated. From these results it is clear that there is a very high natural recovery rate from acute bouts of back pain. Manipulation does not seem to have helped and if anything the patients treated in this way were worse off than those who had the deep heat or indeed deep heat turned down which equated to no treatment at all. In fact statistical analysis did not show that the differences between the various treatment groups were of real significance. It is clear that this study did not find any value in osteopathic manipulation.

The long-term benefits from this type of treatment are even more doubtful. Even if osteopathy were useful it might hasten an improvement likely to occur anyway but not make any real difference in the long run. Equally it cannot protect against future attacks of back pain.

Are there any harmful effects from osteopathy? In the first place back pain can be due to causes other than the type of mechanical problem in which the manipulators specialize. Osteopathic manipulation for ankylosing spondylitis, cancers in the back, and other conditions can do considerable harm. It is always important to be certain that no other condition is present before undergoing such treatment. An osteopath who has not received a broad medical training may miss these other disorders and manipulate when it is contra-indicated. I have seen a patient who had a small tumour in the spine that was responsible for pain; manipulation produced severe damage to the spinal cord and paralysis of the limbs.

The force of manipulation can be quite strong. It is extremely rare that bones are fractured but ligaments can be damaged and some patients can be made worse rather than better by the twisting that is performed.

So there is real doubt about the value of osteopathy. Many patients see osteopaths and are pleased with their improvement following treatment. Others are disappointed or even find themselves worse after the treatment. I would advise that such treatment be given by a medically qualified osteopath. Even under such circumstances it remains uncertain what is being treated, what the treatment actually does to the spine, whether it really does help in the short term and whether there is any long-term benefit. Further careful studies are required in which patients considered suitable for osteopathic treatment should be given this form of manipulation or some other innocuous form of treatment and their progress over succeeding days, weeks, and months studied. The onus is on the osteopaths to conduct these studies, to try to show the value of their forms of treatments and provide more precise guidance as to the types of problems for which they are most suitable.

Chiropractic

At the same time as osteopathy developed, another school concentrating on spinal manipulation grew up and was called chiropractic. According to legend the system was developed by D. D. Palmer, who treated a case of deafness with a sharp thrust to the neck. Chiropractic is based on the belief that poor alignment or partial dislocation of the bones of the neck impinge upon nerves and can be responsible for many types of illness. Manipulation of the neck is thought to correct these mechanical faults and restore body health. Chiropractors believed that their form of manipulation was the treatment not only for spinal pain but also asthma, high blood pressure, migraine, and many other diseases. It is hardly surprising that such claims led to tremendous controversy and considerable doubts about the value of the technique and about its practitioners.

Today most chiropractors concentrate on mechanical problems in the spine and try to forget the exaggerated claims of yesteryear. They believe that joints may either be fixed or displaced beyond their normal ranges of movement, producing various structural and functional changes not only at that site but also in remote tissues, by damaging the nerves. They believe that a poor posture can also be responsible for the symptoms, and that these structural defects can be corrected by manipulation, so making the patient better.

The techniques employed by chiropractors differ from those of osteopaths, who concentrate on twisting the spine by using the shoulders and pelvis as levers. The chiropractor manipulates the vertebrae themselves. The thrust is a rapid but not very powerful force applied directly to the vertebrae. The chiropractor concentrates on determining which type of thrust is appropriate and delivering it with precision.

A major study comparing chiropractic with conventional physiotherapy has recently been published by the Medical Research
Council. Patients with back pain were treated either by a private
chiropractor or in a hospital out-patient physiotherapy clinic.
Immediately after the course of treatment most patients were much
better irrespective of the type of treatment they had received. When
followed-up for periods of up to two years the improvement was
maintained in those who had been treated by the chiropractor but
there was some deterioration in those treated in the hospital
physiotherapy department. These results suggest that chiropractic
has a small but definite advantage over conventional physiotherapy
treatment. This is an important finding but unfortunately the details
of the study have proved extremely controversial. The chiropractic
patients were seen in private by practitioners specializing in spinal
disorders. The physiotherapy patients were seen in conventional
hospital out-patient clinics often by physiotherapists working with
no particular training in back pain. The chiropractic patients
received considerably more treatments than those attending hospital. If chiropractic manipulation was of benefit one would have
expected the major advantage to appear immediately after treatment
rather than appearing gradually over two years. It is possible that
the longer term benefit was due to the greater time and attention the
chiropractor pays to his or her patients and perhaps to more
detailed advice on how to protect the spine against further damage
rather than to any specific effect of chiropractic manipulation.

Nevertheless, this study is important and has had the effect of
stimulating interest in this whole field of manipulation and has
emphasized the need for further careful studies of this type of
treatment.

The status of osteopaths and chiropractors

There has been an interesting divergence in the establishment of
osteopathy and chiropractic in Britain and in the United States of
America. In Britain there are some osteopaths who are medically
qualified. They usually trained as doctors first, became interested in
back pain as a problem, and then learned the techniques and practice
of osteopathy. However, the majory of osteopaths are not
medically qualified but have undergone training in a school of
osteopathy. There are considerably fewer chiropractors than

osteopaths. In general, they are not medically trained but qualified from a college of chiropractors.

In contrast, in the United States the differences between osteopaths and chiropractors have tended to disappear. Many use whichever technique from either profession seems most appropriate for the particular patient. Their training has become increasingly similar to that of medical students and their practice very much like that of general practitioners in this country. They may use drugs and sign medical certificates and indeed some may undertake very little in the way of manipulation. In other words many osteopaths and chiropractors have become another form of doctor. In ordinary clinical care one may be unable to distinguish whether the practitioner had a formal medical training or learned his medicine by these alternative methods. One can readily imagine a new breed of manipulators developing in the United States as the osteopath and chiropractors increasingly become aligned to conventional medicine.

Manipulation by physicians, surgeons, and physiotherapists

Although most doctors do not receive formal training in their student days in the techniques of manipulation, some will learn how to do so and use it for treating back pain patients. There is much controversy about the various forms manipulation can take and about their values. Some doctors may learn osteopathic methods and even attend a special school training physicians in these techniques. Others will learn by postgraduate courses or by working with more experienced colleagues. Although treatment by both medically qualified and lay manipulators can be similar, the advantage of the former is a broad understanding of medicine with the result that other conditions that can masquerade as back pain will not be missed. If one goes to a lay manipulator then almost certainly one will be manipulated. A physician on the other hand would consider alternative diagnoses and other methods of treatment as well as manipulation.

Orthopaedic surgeons will sometimes perform manipulations under anaesthetic. Sometimes they do this with a very light degree of anaesthesia such that the person is half awake. This is particularly helpful when it is uncertain how much back pain is due to damage in the spine and how much to an anxiety state. In the latter the relaxation produced will usually allow much greater freedom of movement. When the patient is completely asleep it is possible to stretch the spine fully and break adhesions limiting the movements of various joints. Orthopaedic surgeons use this technique carefully as sometimes it can stir up trouble rather than relieve pain. In the right person however, it can rapidly improve the movements of a stiff back. However, the majority of manipulations are performed with the patient fully awake so that he can describe the immediate results of the treatment. He will indicate whether the pain has been relieved or the symptoms aggravated. The techniques are constantly modified to provide the best results.

Many physiotherapists learn how to manipulate. Physiotherapists take patients directly as well as by referral from a doctor. The latter ensures that a proper assessment is performed to make sure that nothing serious is being missed and that physiotherapy treatment is appropriate. There are great advantages in close co-operation between physiotherapists and doctors and the two professions work together each exploiting the skills of the other.

Although physiotherapists may learn any of the techniques of manipulation one popular technique is to use the methods described by Geoffrey Maitland, a physiotherapist in Adelaide, Australia. The techniques are colloquially known as Maitland's mobilization and manipulation. The treatment entails repeated visits over several weeks with detailed assessment of the back during each session in order to localize the level responsible for the symptoms and to follow the patient's progress (Plate 8).

The treatments are directed at the particular level of the spine involved, although inevitably they also affect the adjacent levels, and the programme is modified according to progress. The most important component of treatment is mobilization, which consists of oscillatory movement applied manually to the vertebrae. These include rotation and backwards, forwards and side-to-side movements. They may be combined with manipulation techniques which are rapid movements of small amplitude going beyond the normal active ranges of motion. Sometimes traction is added. There may be exercises and occasionally local heat is applied. Although Maitland described the general programme many physiotherapists will modify the treatment according to their own particular beliefs.

Of all the different forms of manipulation only that practised by physiotherapists has been adequately tested by the scientific method. For such a study patients considered suitable for this treatment either receive manipulation or an innocuous type of therapy that superficially appears similar but in fact does not do anything. By comparing the progress of the two groups it is possible to assess the value of the trial treatment.

I would like to describe two such studies with which I was personally concerned. The patients all had back pain. The first study was on back pain patients seeing their general practitioner and with symptoms that persisted long enough for a back X-ray to be requested. The second group had been referred by their general practitioner to hospital rheumatology or orthopaedic clinics for specialist opinions. These patients had more severe and persistent pain with greater disability and more severe X-ray changes. In each study the patients were randomly divided into two groups, one of which received mobilization and manipulation as described by Maitland and given by a physiotherapist who was specially experienced in these techniques. The rest were given a form of deep heat treatment but with the machine turned down so low that no heat was produced. This was given by the same physiotherapist who tried to be as convincing as possible about this form of pseudo-treatment, although she realized it was ineffective. All treatments were given three times a week for as long as necessary up to four weeks. The progress of each patient was assessed by a doctor who did not know which type of treatment was being given. In this way any bias by the patient or by the doctor analysing the results was minimized.

In the general practitioner study, the majority of patients, whether receiving manipulation or not, were much improved after the four-week treatment period. However, those who received Maitland's mobilization and manipulation were slightly better than the rest. Two months later most patients were still improved but the differences between the two groups had largely disappeared. At final follow-up after a year the progress of the two groups was identical. By contrast, in the hospital series, most patients were also improved after the four-week treatment period although they had not done as well as in the general practitioner study. This was expected as these patients had much more severe back problems. However, there was absolutely no difference in progress between those receiving manipulation or not. Similarly two months later and at one year the progress of the two sub-groups was identical.

Information from the two studies was analysed very carefully. The conclusions were (a) that most episodes of back pain will get better; (b) that in those likely to improve, manipulation can hasten the process to a limited extent but it makes no difference in the long run ; (c) that although some patients seemed to do well immediately after a mobilization and manipulation session other patients had similar improvement after a pseudo-treatment session. We even had one or two who came back asking for a further course of the pseudo-treatment when they developed another attack of back pain some time later. The patients in the hospital series had more severe problems and in these we failed to find any benefit from mobilization and manipulation. Several further studies have been performed tackling this problem in the UK and North America. Some failed to show any benefit at all; others had similar results to my own.

So where does this leave mobilization and manipulation by physiotherapists? Most people will get better anyway. The treatment will accelerate improvement in a few. The personal attention and interest of the physiotherapist will play an enormous part in accelerating recovery. This will be dealt with in more detail with regard to the psychology of back pain in Chapter 12. The advice and instruction on the use and care of the back given during the treatment sessions is very helpful in avoiding future relapses. However, the real value of the procedures themselves remains doubtful.

The evidence in favour of mobilization and manipulation is weak. It suggests that it may have some temporary benefit but makes no difference in the long term. No clear evidence has been produced in favour of osteopathic manipulation but there is the controversial study about some longer term advantage for chiropractic. The use of a comparison of the results of manipulation with patients who have not received any particular form of manipulation is remarkably chastening. In my own studies, if we had only treated patients with mobilization and manipulation and had not included the comparison groups, we would have reported that about three quarters of our patients got better and said clearly that the treatment was dramatically effective. We know that this was not so, but simply that the natural powers of recovery of the back may be helped a small fraction by manipulation. It is now up to osteopaths, chiropractors, physiotherapists, and doctors who manipulate, to prove that their forms of treatment are effective. The challenge is there.

Should one seek manipulation?

So the position with respect to manipulation is very confused. Who should be manipulated? What techniques should be used? Should the manipulation be by physicians specializing in manipulative medicine, orthopaedic surgeons, physiotherapists, osteopaths, or chiropractors? Does it do any good? The evidence on these points has been presented and it is clear that the answers to these questions are not easy.

In the first place, one must be certain that the back pain is caused by a mechanical problem and not by some other disease that may be missed. Manipulation under such circumstances can be an absolute disaster. Bones may break, ligaments tear, and nerves be severely damaged, producing paralysis. A careful medical assessment is an essential preliminary and should be performed by a doctor who has the training to recognize these other causes of back pain. The diagnosis should be reviewed from time to time because a condition may not be obvious at its onset but becomes clear as time passes. In the straightforward case, careful examination and laboratory tests may seem a waste of time; their importance lies in identifying the unusual problem and avoiding the wrong treatment.

Most attacks of back pain will get better with the more conservative forms of treatment already described. Manipulation may be tried but in my view the decision should be made by people with a medical training. After all, if one goes to an osteopath or chiropractor, one is seeking manipulation—one has already made the decision that one wants manipulation. Apart from the most exceptional circumstances that is what is given. Surely the patient should seek the best treatment, of which manipulation is only one of the options available? A balanced view of all the forms of treatment available is required.

Does manipulation do any good?

The lack of information and doubts about the possible values of manipulation have already been expressed. We hear many anecdotal stories of immediate recovery after manipulation but also of many others who failed to improve and some who are made worse. The evidence available suggests that most attacks of back pain will get better anyway; manipulation at best can hasten this in a few. The many different forms of manipulation and types of manipulators create further problems. We simply do not know if any one form of treatment is any better or worse than others. Further proper scientifically controlled trials are urgently required to answer these questions.

So in my view a medical assessment is essential and the decision about this form of treatment should only be made by someone with all the skills required. The value of manipulation remains very uncertain and we simply do not know whether one form of manipulation may prove of real value. The results of further work trying out these various forms of treatment are eagerly awaited.

Lumbar corsets and spinal supports

If the back hurts when moved then holding it still in some form of splint should relieve the symptoms. This simple concept has lead to the use of a wide variety of spinal jackets and various types of spinal brace and lumbar corsets for back pain. Although apparently helpful in relieving symptoms, today there is considerable scepticism about the use of corsets particularly for the less severe forms of backache. Although they are helpful immediately, they produce stiffness of the back and in the long run may cause more harm than good.

The most effective way of splinting the spine is by using some form of jacket moulded around the whole trunk. Such jackets used to be made of plaster-of-Paris with wet plaster-of-Paris bandages wrapped over a body stocking. They set within a few minutes to form a solid shell. This type of jacket is very effective in stopping the back from moving but it is extremely heavy, hot, and physically uncomfortable. Today we use modern lightweight materials but nevertheless there are obvious difficulties with hygiene and washing, so this type of jacket can only be worn for a relatively short period of time.

On the other hand, spinal corsets are very widely used (see Plate 9). In Great Britain in one year about 400 000 lumbar corsets were prescribed under the National Health Service. This does not take into account corsets obtained privately or by patients themselves.

This means that the total must be a staggering half million or so. Interestingly, corsets are prescribed twice as frequently in England than in Scotland. We do not known why this is—perhaps Scots are hardier.

There are many different manufacturers of lumbar corsets. They all make them to a common basic pattern but with considerable variation in style, form, material, and fastenings. They all contain a strong strengthening pad which stretches from the sacrum to the mid-back, is encased within a firm body belt, and tied around the abdomen. Most corsets use steel strips to provide the actual support and these are moulded to the shape of the patient's back. A recent design uses a heat-mouldable plastic pad. This is heated to 70° C and moulded to the patient's back. On cooling it retains this shape but sets extremely firm. The pad is inserted in a special pocket in the back of the corset. The material of the corset is made of various types of cloth or even canvas. It must be strong to allow the corset to be drawn tight. For people who tend to get too hot, or for use in hot climates, there is a version available with multiple perforations which allow air to circulate. The corset is drawn tight with laces, straps, or special Velcro fastenings.

Wearing a corset will relieve pain in the back but does nothing for the underlying problem, so it is only a form of palliation. Indeed, it can do harm, as the muscles can become weak with lack of use, and sometimes prolonged wearing of a corset can lead to the 'stuck back' described earlier. Corsets should be worn only for short periods, not indefinitely. When someone is starting to get going after a severe episode of back pain, and perhaps after being confined to bed, then the lumbar corset may help him to start moving around without upsetting his back. A corset should be worn for perhaps a couple of weeks or so and then discarded. A corset may also be worn for a few days to help the patient over a mild attack of pain. However, it is all too easy for a patient to become addicted to wearing the corset and find it impossible to discard. The patient continues wearing the corset for years and because of its use develops a stiff and painful back. Some corsets are poorly made and fall to bits within a few weeks. On the whole I think this is a good thing because it prevents the patient becoming too used to wearing the corset and needing to wear it indefinitely.

There are several theories as to how corsets relieve pain. The first is simply that they limit the movements of the back. Although a considerable amount of back movements can still be performed despite wearing the corset, it does appear that the limitation of the back movements is important. The second is that the tightness of the corset raises the pressure within the abdomen so allowing it to transmit some of the body load and therefore decreasing the body load on the spine, as described in Chapter 1. Another possibility is that the corset is simply acting as a warm body belt much like thermal underwear or the warm cummerbund described earlier. Finally a tight corset may stimulate nerves in the back so relieving the sensation of pain in a similar way to acupuncture and transcutaneous nerve stimulation as described in the next chapter. All these mechanisms combine together to provide relief.

6

Pain and its control

Introduction

Although we all know what pain is, it is almost impossible to describe it adequately in words. It is an unpleasant type of sensation produced by injury or disease. We feel pain in our minds although we locate it in the affected part of the body. Without the conscious mind, pain would not exist, only a variety of electrical and chemical impulses.

Although pain is unpleasant it does serve an important purpose. It provides a warning that tissues are being damaged so that the subject can take appropriate action. If this ability to perceive pain is lost, injuries may occur without the subject being aware of it. Extreme cases of this are seen in certain neurological diseases in which loss of pain sensation in the fingers may allow them to be burned by cigarettes, or, if feeling is lost in the feet, poorly fitting shoes may rub and produce nasty ulcers.

One approach to the problem of back pain is not to worry too much about what is wrong with the back but simply to try to control the sensation of pain. In its simplest form, we use pain-relieving medicines like aspirin. However, modern advances in the understanding of the physiology of pain sensation are not only providing us with insight into how traditional forms of treatment may work but also leading to the development of new methods of pain control.

Pain-relieving medicines, analgesics and anti-inflammatory drugs

Medicines that relieve pain are known as analgesics. They are often used for people with back pain and the particular ones prescribed will depend upon the severity and nature of the symptoms. In the patient with really severe back pain and sciatica, perhaps due to a burst intervetebral disc, very strong analgesics may be required. Sometimes even pethidine, morphine, or related drugs are used if they are the only drugs powerful enough to provide adequate relief of pain. There is a risk of addiction with medicines such as these. They have an obvious and important role for people dying from some very painful illnesses but doctors do not like using them, for treating a non-fatal condition such as back pain. They are therefore used very sparingly, restricted to the most severe cases, withdrawn after a very short period of time, and replaced by simpler analgesics. However, recent research has shown that natural morphine-like substances are formed within the brain and play an important role in controlling the actual experience of pain. More of this later.

Some analgesics are pain relievers alone but others also can reduce inflammation. These are known as non-steroidal anti-inflammatory analgesics. This means that they are not cortisone-like drugs and they can control inflammation as well as relieving pain. Although the anti-inflammatory effect is most obviously useful in inflammatory diseases like rheumatoid arthritis, there is an element of inflammation in many back problems so that, on the whole, these drugs are more valuable than pure pain relievers.

The doctor can decide whether pure pain relievers or the non-steroidal anti-inflammatory tablets are more likely to help. Some patients find that they become very stiff when they rest. They may have difficulty getting out of a chair and take a little while to get going. They feel very stiff when they wake up in the morning and this may last anything from a few minutes to an hour or so. Once they are moving around they are not too bad with an increasing activity they then develop further pain. Their problems are somewhat similar to those of patients with ankylosing spondylitis which is described in Chapter 10. It is likely that they have some mild inflammatory damage in the spine perhaps as a result of the mechanical problems. These patients tend to do better with the anti-inflammatory analgesic drugs. On the other hand the patient whose pain eases during and after a period of resting but returns on physical exertion is more likely to be helped by a pure analgesic.

The most well known of the non-steroidal anti-inflammatory pain-relieving drugs is aspirin, which is technically known as acetyl salicylic acid. This drug was first extracted from the willow tree or salix—hence the name salicylates. Aspirin is a useful drug and is quite good at relieving pain. However, its effects last only a few hours and it may be necessary to take three tables four times a day, or even more to control the symptoms properly.

There is no medicine known that is without risk of possible side-effects. If one thinks about it this is hardly surprising, because in order to be effective drugs must alter the ways in which cells and tissues in the body behave and such changes, if taken to excess, are likely to be harmful. Aspirin is no exception but fortunately, on the whole, it is a very safe drug. Many tons of aspirin are consumed per year and only a few people come to real harm. However, aspirin can upset some people. The commonest problem is indigestion due to irritation of the stomach lining. Some patients may lose blood, either as a very slow process which may gradually produce anaemia or very occasionally as a sudden internal haemorrhage. An excessive intake of aspirin may cause ringing noises in the ears and even deafness, which improve once the dose is reduced.

In order to make the drug more acceptable aspirin is often presented in other forms. Perhaps the most popular is aspirin which can be dissolved in water. Sometimes the tablet has a special coating to prevent irritation of the stomach lining. It may be mixed or combined with other medicines in an effort to enhance its actions and to reduce some of the stomach upsets. Commonly I prescribe simple soluble aspirin, as many of the other preparations, particularly the extremely expensive forms sold under various brand names, have relatively little advantage over it.

If aspirin produces stomach upset, paracetamol is a useful alternative. It is not quite as effective a pain reliever as aspirin but carries less risk of an abdominal upset and for that reason is preferred by many people. Many of the preparations available contain mixtures of aspirin and paracetamol. There is one interesting compound in which the two are chemically combined and only separate once the drug is absorbed into the body, so providing dual benefit and avoiding some of the stomach problems of aspirin.

In an effort to improve on the performance of these pain-relieving compounds pharmaceutical companies have developed a whole new range of drugs, which are very similar to each other. Many of these compounds are related in their structure to propionic acid, and include ibuprofen (Brufen), naproxen (Naprosyn), keto-profen (Orudis), diclofenac (Volatrol), azapropazone (Rheumox), piroxican (Feldene), and many others. The stimulus for their development was the need to control inflammation in diseases such as rheumatoid arthritis. However, they are also useful for back troubles and are often prescribed. They are as good or even slightly better than aspirin in relieving pain but have advantages in that they produce fewer stomach upsets, and fewer tablets have to be taken each day. Ibuprofen has proved a very safe drug and is now available from chemist shops without the need for a doctor's prescription. Some anti-inflammatory drugs are available as creams that can be rubbed into the painful area of the back two or three times a day.

Indomethacin (Indocid) is a more effective pain relieving anti-inflammatory drug than those mentioned so far. However, it does carry a somewhat greater risk of unwanted effects. These include abdominal upsets of various sorts. In addition, indomethacin can produce very unpleasant headaches and a feeling of muzziness. For these reasons this drug is usually reserved for more severe back problems when other medicines do not have sufficient effect.

Pure pain relieving drugs that have no anti-inflammatory properties are sometimes used. The more potent ones are available only on a doctor's prescription and include dihydrocodeine (DF118) and dextropropoxyphyene, the latter is often prescribed mixed with paracetamol and is know as Co-proxamol or Distalgesic and familiarly called 'DGs'.

It is not possible to give a comprehensive account listing all the possible drugs as there is such a wide range available. However, the majority are anti-inflammatory pain relieving drugs or just pure pain relieving drugs related to those that have been described.

The way the tablets are taken depends upon the nature of the back problem. If the patient is continuously in pain then he should take them regularly throughout the day. If the pain is worse at any particular time of day then the medicine should be timed to be taken, say half or one hour before. Some people have a great deal of pain in bed at night. The first thing to do is to improve the bed, but, if this is not adequate, then a large dose of pain relieving medicines last thing before going to sleep may prove the answer. Many of these tablets are effective only for three or four hours, which means their benefits will have worn off by the early hours of the morning. There are now longer-acting tablets and also slow-release preparations available that lengthen the duration of action. One of these tablets taken last thing at night, usually with a glass of milk to avoid upsetting the stomach, will allow a comfortable night and prevent the morning stiffness. Some of these medicines work for 24 hours and need only be taken once a day.

Another alternative which is aesthetically unappealing but which can be remarkably effective is to take the medicine in the form of a suppository. The chemicals are absorbed only very slowly from the back passage so that they work over a long period. Suppositories have another advantage in that they reduce the risk of abdominal upsets. For the person who suffers from severe indigestion, suppositories may be the answer. If I think a suppository may help I usually ask the patient to give them a try for a few days and then to discard them if they find the technique unacceptable or ineffective. The vast majority are so pleased with the results that they are happy to continue.

Other medicines for pain relief

Unfortunately the analgesic and anti-inflammatory medicines described do not help everybody. Although they work for most people, for some they are not effective. Therefore analysis of the types of pain may suggest other ways of obtaining relief. A careful study of the nature of the problem is necessary.

In very acute backache there is often a lot of spasm of the back muscles. They contract extremely hard pulling the back often to one side or the other to reduce the pressure on damaged tissues. This spasm can itself be a very painful process. Indeed these painful spasms may induce more spasm so that a vicious circle develops with severe pain and this secondary spasm may become the principal cause of symptoms rather than the original back injury. Medicines are now available which will reduce the muscle spasms. They were intially developed for patients with various kinds of neurological disease such as stroke in which nerves are over-stimulated producing excessive muscle contractions. These medicines also enable the acute back patient with a lot of muscle spasm to get over the attack much more rapidly.

Pain relief for patients with severe persistent chronic back pain is a difficult problem. Many suffer widespread pain often spreading up into the neck and into the limbs and may have a burning or pins and needles sensation in the skin in a widespread area. The back may be extremely tender and even light pressure can sometimes produce severe pain. In such patients ordinary analgesics and anti-inflammatory drugs are commonly useless. Small doses of certain drugs, which are usually prescribed by psychiatrists treating depression, may be effective. In particular, amitriptyline and a number of medicines related to it can be useful. Psychiatrists use quite large doses in order to obtain the appropriate benefit. However, for back pain patients only very small doses of these medicines are usually necessary. In prescribing this type of treatment I often have to reassure the patient that I do not think that they are depressed nor am I aiming to treat depression. It is simply that these medicines in small doses can block the passage of the pain sensation through the spinal cord and relieve many of the symptoms.

Some chronic back sufferers describe neuralgic types of pain. They develop severe shooting or electric shock pains spreading down from the back into one or other leg. It appears that the nerves are much more sensitive than normal and discharge producing this type of pain. The drugs used for treating epilepsy may be helpful in this situation. In epilepsy, patients develop fits because the cells in the brain are over sensitive and suddenly discharge producing convulsions. Anti-epileptic drugs calm down these nerve cells and stop the fits from happening. Similarly in these back problems the nerve cells in the spine are oversensitive and discharge producing severe shooting pains in the legs. The same types of drugs can calm down the spine nerve cells and reduce or stop this type of pain.

All the medicines described in this section can be helpful but a careful analysis is necessary to decide when they are appropriate. They all affect the nerves and muscles and as a result can make the patient feel rather sleepy. They are usually started in small doses and then the dose slowly increased in order to obtain the desired effect. Sometimes they may make the patient feel sleepy during the day even on a small dose but usually this will wear off in a few days. I encourage patients to bear with it if at all possible. Care should be taken about driving because obviously the treatment might slow their reactions. Their effects are also increased by alcohol and again patients should be careful about drinking at the same time as starting on these tablets particularly if driving.

The perception of pain

For countless centuries opium has been used as a drug of addiction. Opium is derived from a certain species of poppy. The poppies grown in this country do not produce the drug but the seed pods of a special variety known as *Papaver somniferum*, which grows in warmer climates, produce quite large amounts. The drug may be taken by mouth but quite commonly it is smoked. A pipe is passed from person to person in communal sessions. The drug has a calming and relaxing effect and removes many anxieties. Frequent use may lead to dependence on the drug, a requirement for greater quantities, and eventually to addiction. Use of opium and drugs derived from it is outlawed in most countries of the world. Although the basic constitutents are remarkably easy to produce and extremely cheap, on the black market the drug costs many hundreds or even thousands times its true value.

The active substance in opium that provides its effects is morphine. By simple chemical manipulation an even more potent substance, dimethyl morphine or heroin may be made. These compounds would be of purely legal interest but for the fact that they are the most potent pain-relieving substances known. They are effective in relieving severe pain when commonplace drugs such as aspirin have failed. Morphine and related chemicals are used for people suffering from severe pain, and particularly if they have a fatal illness. The most common of these is widespread cancer. Often they are used after operations when the need is to relieve pain for only a short period. The use of these drugs is always balanced against the potential risk of producing addiction and if this seems at all likely then extreme care is required.

All of this may seem of academic interest with regard to back pain, as the majority of sufferers do not have sufficiently severe symptoms to merit the use of such drugs. However, in recent years, there have been fascinating discoveries of how the brain perceives the sensation of pain and we have now come to realize that morphine-like substances are formed naturally within the brain and control our normal experience of pain.

Until very recently, ideas of pain perception had changed little over countless centuries. The common idea was that a stimulus felt peripherally such as a burn or a cut would stimulate special receptors in the skin which would convey a message along the nerves right up to the brain, thus producing the sensation of pain. The system was seen as a bit like a telephone line with a single wire that conveyed this special message—pain. Although this explanation accorded with the anatomical descriptions of the pathways of the nerves, nevertheless is failed to explain all the problems. Some of us may find a certain injury painful whereas others may tolerate it without significant discomfort. In other words we may have a low or high threshold to painful stimuli. Perhaps this just reflects the sort of people that we are. Some of us feel pain more readily than others. However, there is more to it than this as on some occasions we may find a particular stimulus excrutiatingly painful yet on other occasions we may barely notice it. Perhaps the most graphic examples of this are soldiers in the heat of battle or boxers during a fight, who may receive severe injuries and yet not notice them and continue fighting. It is only some time after the fight that they realize their injuries and feel pain.

David Livingstone, the nineteenth-century explorer in Africa, provided a remarkably vivid account of an incident very suggestive of a similar phenomenon. Livingstone was standing alone on a small grassy hill when he was suddenly attacked by a large male lion. He wrote:

I heard a shout. Staring and looking half round, I saw the lion just in the act of springing upon me. I was on a little height; he caught my shoulder as he sprang and we both came to the ground below together. Growling horribly close to my ear, he shook me as a terrier does a rat. The shock produced a stupor similar to that which seems to be felt by a mouse after the first shake of a cat. It caused a sort of dreaminess in which there was no sense of pain nor feeling of terror, although quite conscious of all that was happening. It was like what patients partially under the influence of chloroform describe, who see all the operation but feel not the knife. This singular condition was not the result of any mental process. The shake annihilated fear, and allowed no sense of horror in looking round at the beast. The peculiar state is probably produced in all animals killed by carnivora; and if so, it is a merciful provision by our benevolent Creator for lessening the pain of death. (Livingstone (1872) *Adventures and discoveries in the interior of Africa*. Hubbard, Philadelphia.)

Livingstone is describing in himself and in animals an inappropriate tranquillity and lack of feeling of pain, while being literally eaten alive. This has often been observed in animals and ascribed to 'a state of shock' without any real understanding of what has happened.

A simple telephone-line theory of pain-transmission cannot explain what is going on here. A certain stress should always produce the same unpleasant sensation and this would not be prevented by the circumstances in which the injury occurred.

Thus there seems to be some mechanism within the brain by which the sensation of pain can be suppressed in appropriate circumstances. This ability to suffer injury and not experience pain during periods of stress allows the subject to perform tasks or undertake procedures that otherwise he would be unable to do. The short-term advantage is that the soldier or boxer can fight on despite injury (although in the long run more harm than good may be achieved as pain usually provides a warning that should be heeded).

This phenomenon was regarded as little more than a curiosity until the late 1960s, when experiments were performed on animals in which parts of the brain were stimulated using minute electric currents, in the search for the various centres that control certain types of sensation. The particular one being sought was that responsible for pleasure. How fortunate we would be if by switching on this current we could stimulate such a centre in the brain and feel happy and contented! During the course of these experiments the scientists found that stimulating a certain part of the brain made the animal unresponsive to a painful stimulus although in other respects it remained normal. This discovery was applied to man and used for patients with severe pain uncontrollable by simpler means. The most common cause of this is extensive cancer. When electrodes were placed in the appropriate part of the brain and electrically stimulated there was a fading away of the pain. Nevertheless the patients remained fully awake and alert. Other sensations such as touch remained normal and the patients had full control over their bodily movements. These electrodes were tried in various regions and it was found that the most effective site was in the mid-brain around the so-called central canal. The site was identical in both animals and in man.

This technique has been so successful that in some centres it is in use as a clinical form of pain control. The electrodes are placed in the right spot by insertion through a needle under three-dimensional X-ray control. They are left there permanently with the leads led away under the surface of the skin. Repeated electrical stimulation may be required. In some people they may be effective in controlling the pain for years. Although they do nothing to affect the cancer, this technique may well make the final period of the patient's life comfortable.

At the same time as this work was being developed, further research was undertaken on morphine and drugs related to it. In particular it was found that by a relatively trivial modification of the morphine molecule, a compound called nalorphine could be developed that blocked the effect of morphine itself. If it was given prior to morphine then the pain-relieving and other effects of morphine would disappear. This is not just a scientific curiosity but indicates that within the brain there is a very specific receptor to which morphine and allied drugs will attach to produce their effects. When a compound that is similar but not quite the same is given first, it can attach itself without producing morphine-like effects and prevent the morphine molecule from subsquently combining with the same receptor.

The search was on to find where morphine and its blocking agent worked. It is possible to attach markers to molecules so that we can identify what happens to them inside the body. In the case of morphine this is a radioactive hydrogen atom which replaces one of the hydrogen atoms that is normally present in the molecule. By giving the labelled drug to an animal it is then possible to seek out where the label ends up. Radio-labelled morphine was found in precisely the same area in the midbrain, around the central canal, where electrical stimulation gave pain relief.

The precise coincidence of these two areas was too much to accept as a chance finding. It suggested that the two were inherently related to each other. The possibility was raised that morphine works by binding to particular receptor sites in that region of the brain. Moreover, the electrical stimulation releases a morphine-like substance within that particular area and that is why this technique is able to produce profound control of painful sensation. This implies that the brain itself is able to make a morphine-like substance. The next step was to try to find the actual material and in 1975 workers in Scotland for the first time identified morphine-like material in the brain and called it enkephalin. We now know that there is not a single morphine-like substance but a number of substances known as endorphins and that they are principally formed in this particular area of the brain and spinal cord.

It has become apparent that there is a very complex system for controlling the sensation of pain. Not only will peripheral damage give rise to impulses that travel up the nerves to the brain to produce this sensation but also the brain itself has a mechanism for modulating the actual sensation experienced. Even this system has its complications and today our understanding of the subject is still rapidly expanding. We now know that there are fibres in the spinal cord that will preferentially stimulate the pain-controlling centre and prevent the sensation of pain. There are also fibres that descend from the pain-suppression centre down the spinal cord and will control the transmission of impulses between the nerves and the spinal cord itself. There are receptors in the spinal cord that respond to endorphins of the same sort as in the brain. In addition pain producing and pain relieving substances are formed and released in the spinal cord. These may sensitize or desensitize the nerve cells so that the whole central nervous system responds in complicated ways in producing the sensation of pain; the nature of the response varies widely between different people.

The pain signal within the spinal cord can spread to involve nerves that do not have any direct connection with the injured part. Thus some patients experience pain over a much wider area than would be expected simply from the nature of the original injury. It is likely that this is happening in many patients with severe chronic back pain. The original problem may have been a herniated (slipped) disc affecting a single nerve but subsequently the symptoms seem to be coming from areas that should have nothing to do with the original nerve injury. This problem is most marked in the patient with arachnoiditis in whom there is severe scarring around the nerves with multiple damage and the problem is compounded by this spread of the pain signal within the spinal cord producing severe and widespread symptoms.

We now understand much more about how morphine can produce such profound control of pain. It is not simply a compound derived from the poppy that happens to be a pain reliever. It is a substance that mimics a naturally occurring material within the nervous system and that is why it has such profound effects. This suggests that the variability of pain actually experienced may be due to altered release of endorphins which occurs irrespective of the severity of the actual injury. If we can find ways of triggering the release of the naturally occurring endorphins then we may have a mechanism of pain relief that mimics that naturally occurring in the body.

Some of the pain-relieving methods that at first sight do not seem to have a proper scientific basis could well work by this mechanism. To take a simple example, if a child injures his leg his mother may be able to 'rub it better'. What happens when she does this? It seems very unlikely that the rubbing can do anything for the injury itself. We believe that the rubbing stimulates certain nerves that run to the spinal cord and from there up to the pain controlling centre in the midbrain and release the morphine-like substance, so providing relief of the symptoms.

Such stimulation of the skin produces impulses that carry messages in nerves in both thin and thick fibres. Only the thin fibres convey the pain message but impulses in the larger fibres can block the perception of the painful element of the sensation. This is known as the gate control theory of pain. There is a 'gate' which is either open to allow pain to be felt or closed by stimulation of these large nerve fibres so that the pain disappears. It is a bit like a signal from a jamming station blocking reception of a radio broadcast. Many forms of treatment may work by closing the gate. These include massage, friction, mustard baths, ointments that produce some irritation of the skin, transcutaneous nerve stimulation (see p. 107), and even acupuncture. A fundamental readjustment of our ideas of pain control is well underway.

The study of pain-controlling mechanisms has also influenced our understanding of the placebo response. A placebo is a drug or other kind of treatment which mimics a standard procedure under trial but in effect does nothing. Many back pain sufferers will seemingly respond well to a placebo, although the benefits generally are transitory. In the past, the response to a placebo has usually been taken as an indication of the lack of any serious underlying problem. It was assumed that if someone got better when in truth nothing had been done then the problem was all in the mind and nothing serious was wrong in the first place. However, this is a gross oversimplification. A series of patients who had undergone surgery were given a placebo which basically was a medicine totally lacking in effect, and half of them also received the morphine-blocking substance nalophine. The pain was considerably worse in the group receiving nalorphine than in those receiving placebo alone. This suggests that the placebo is doing something positive and can relieve pain by causing the release of morphine-like endorphins in the brain. The placebo benefit was blocked by the nalorphine in those receiving this drug.

Can endorphins be given by mouth and will they relieve pain and be useful for backache? The drug companies are developing research programmes along these lines. Already synthetic endorphins are available and have been found capable of producing profound pain relief when injected around the spinal cord. The latest compounds look promising for oral administration but it is still very early days to know how effective they will be, whether they will be useful for back pain and whether any complications may arise.

So there the matter rests at the present time. We are begining to appreciate how the central nervous system itself is able to alter the subjective experience of the sensation of pain by controlled release of endorphins. This knowledge is leading to new ideas on pain control.

Acupuncture

Acupuncture has been the subject of controversy for many years. It was used by the Chinese as a method of pain relief and to control a wide variety of different diseases. Until very recently acupuncture was totally disregarded by Western medicine as unscientific and valueless. However, more enquiring approaches have provided support for a pain-relieving action under certain circumstances.

Techniques of acupuncture have been used since pre-history and there are records of acupuncture on bone etchings from about 1600 BC. The first detailed description in ancient Chinese literature was in *The Yellow Emperor's Book of Internal Medicine* written between 400 and 200 BC. This book is written as a dialogue between the Yellow Emperor and a physician but probably respresents a collection of teachings from around that time. The Yellow Emperor himself is believed to have lived at around 250 BC. The ancient Chinese believed in the principle of Tao—the Way— which was responsible for creating order out of chaos and the harmonious coexistence of good and evil. They believed in a vital essence or life force which they called Ch'i. This force might be called life energy and flows through all living things and is essential to their well-being. Ch'i is a balanced mixture of two opposing forces known as Yin and Yang. Yin is the negative, feminine, and passive force, while Yang is positive, masculine, and active. Examples of Yin things are night, autumn or winter, cold, and the moon, and Yang things are day, spring or summer, heat, and the sun. However, Yin and Yang are not exclusive but coexist and blend with each other in complex ways.

The Ch'i or life force was believed to flow around the body through ducts, the lines of which were known as Meridians. There were twelve principal Meridians divided into two groups. One group of Meridians is Yang and is connected to the hollow organs of the body concerned with nutrition and excretion such as the gall bladder, the intestine, and the bladder. The other Meridians are Yin and are related to the solid organs concerned with circulation of the blood such as the heart, lungs, liver, spleen, and kidney. The life force circulates through the Meridians in a definite order and at particular times of day and if the circulation is stopped or out of balance then sickness or death can result.

Detailed examination of the pulse at the wrist will tell whether there is any imbalance between the Meridians. The pulse in each hand is felt in three positions and palpated first with a very light superficial pressure and then with a much former grasp. This produces a total of twelve pulses and each will reflect problems in a different bodily organ. Analysis of the pulses is used to indicate what is wrong and to help in choosing the site for insertion of the acupuncture needles.

When it is known which Meridian is abnormal, the flow of Ch'i is corrected by inserting the needle in the acupuncture point on the Meridian. Complex charts were drawn by the ancient Chinese physicians showing not only these principal Meridians but other less important lines and showing the appropriate acupuncture sites for various disorders (Plate 10).

The traditional acupuncture needle was made of gold or silver and was of varying lengths, thicknesses, and shapes of point. Different schools of acupuncture inserted them at various depths. They could be inserted quickly or slowly, removed immediately or left in place, withdrawn, and re-inserted, and rotated clockwise or anti-clockwise, quickly or slowly. Some even put a blob of inflammable material known as moxa on the end of the needle. When lit it burned slowly and heated the needle and the skin. This is known as moxibustion.

Some patients were treated only once and others daily. It is not clear whether these variations made any difference. Acupuncture was used for a wide variety of different disorders including not only back pain but also heart troubles, migraine, toothache, painful periods, and many other problems.

An interesting variant developed by French and Chinese acupuncturists was known as auricullo-therapy or ear acupuncture. According to the proponents of this system, the whole body is represented upside-down on the surface of the ear. By palpating the ear and today, by using electrical tests, they believe they can diagnose which part of the body is abnormal. This area is treated by acupuncture. Others examine and treat the sole of the foot in the same way.

Acupuncture is still frequently used for back pain although its real value remains in doubt. Although many patients will claim relief of pain after this treatment the evidence obtained by comparing patients treated properly and by sham or incorrect acupuncture techniques has shown that there is little, if any, advantage for those treated in the official acupuncturist's manner. It may be that the precise site of insertion of the acupuncture needles does not matter too much, so that correctly or incorrectly performed acupuncture may still provide the same beneift. Perhaps it is the needling that counts irrespective of the ancient Chinese theories. If the technique works, and it does seem to help in some people, it provides only temporary pain relief but will not alter the underlying fault and is not of long-term value. In those who benefit, the relief from pain may last anything from a few hours to several weeks.

Today acupuncturists often use stainless steel needles. The needles must be properly sterilized to avoid transmitting disease. Acupuncturists often stick to the traditional acupuncture sites although many do this out of custom rather than belief. Sometimes they measure the electrical resistance of the skin, as alterations are thought to indicate where the needles are best inserted. Others may use the traditional sites indicated by pulse diagnosis. An examination may be made for tender trigger spots and the needles inserted there (Plate 11). Stimulation is performed by either rotating the needle or sometimes by passing a small electric current. Patients may report a sensation called 'take' derived from the Chinese word 'Te-Ch'i which is a numb sensation developing around the acupuncture site. When a 'take' occurs the results are likely to be good.

There are various theories about how acupuncture can relieve pain. One idea is that it is simply a form of hypnotic suggestion and that the procedure itself is relatively unimportant. It is more likely that the needling stimulates the large nerve fibres that travel up to the spinal cord and brain and will block the transmission of pain impulses conducted through small nerve fibres, so closing the 'gate' described earlier. When acupuncture is carried out in an area previously rendered devoid of sensation by infiltrating with local anaesthetic, the pain-relieving action of the acupuncture itself was lost. Acupuncture could cause the release of endorphins in the midbrain, so preventing perception of pain. It is a fascinating discovery that the relief of pain by acupuncture is abolished by the morphine-blocking drug nalorphine. If endorphins are released in the midbrain by acupuncture it is fortunate that they are non-addictive as otherwise we might well find vast numbers of people totally committed to acupunctural stimulation. The successful treatment by acupuncture of withdrawal symptoms in some cases of heroin and morphine addiction may well work in this way.

So the current evidence is that acupuncture can provide relief of pain. It is probably the needling that counts and the precise site is relatively unimportant. However, the method will only give temporary relief of symptoms and not for everybody. Although of some help it is not satisfactory in the long-term management of the back pain problem.

Transcutaneous nerve stimulation

Pain relief from acupuncture arises by stimulation of the skin. Because of the physical difficulty in inserting needles, an electrical method known as transcutaneous nerve stimulation or TNS has been developed. Tiny pulses of electricity are applied to the skin with the aim of stimulating the large nerve fibres and closing the 'gate' in the brain, so preventing the passage of pain impulses and relieving the sensation of pain.

The apparatus consists of a small portable case containing a battery and controls with leads connected to electrodes which are attached to the body. The skin is cleaned thoroughly and dried. The electrode pads are covered with a special electrically conducting jelly and taped to the skin. Controls on the stimulator will adjust the severity of each impulse, the frequency with which they occur, and the length of time that each impulse lasts. The pulses are felt as pricking sensations and the controls adjusted to provide the most comfortable level. The site of the pain will usually determine where the electrodes should be fixed. Often it is a matter of trial and error to determine where they are most effective. The stimulator is worn on a belt or carried in a pocket and the patient can carry on with normal activities and simply switch on the apparatus whenever the need arises (Plate 12). The actual current flowing is minute and cannot produce burns or any local damage. However, there is a risk in people with heart pacemakers as the electrical pulses may interfere with their function. In general they are inadvisable for such patients. In people with other types of heart disease they can affect the heart rhythm and they should be used only after careful evaluation.

Some patients can obtain remarkable relief of pain by TNS and after each burst of impulses this may last anything from a few minutes up to several days. It is often difficult to know who will benefit and in a comparison between TNS and a sham device for sufferers from intractable low back pain there was no real advantage for the stimulator. However some people are convinced that they are helped and for them this is good enough.

This is still a rapidly advancing field with improvements in techniques constantly appearing. I am sure that we can look forward to considerable developments in this type of approach to pain control.

7

Injections and operations

This chapter is about highly specialized forms of treatment for back pain. They require very careful assessment of the back problem by skilled physicians and surgeons who are practised in the various techniques. In general, injections and operations are reserved for more severe back problems when simpler forms of treatment have not worked.

Injections for low back pain

Injections are used in several different ways for low back pain sufferers. They may be made into trigger points, into the epidural space, or directly into the intervertebral disc.

Trigger points and fibrositic nodules

Some patients have well-defined very tender areas in the back. They are best identified by carefully feeling the back with the patient lying on his stomach. Often a small firm nodule can be felt in the muscle. These nodules can be exquisitely tender and pressing on them makes the back pain very much worse. When the right area is found, the patient will make it known in no uncertain fashion.

These tender areas are known as trigger points, as pressure triggers the symptoms; they are sometimes called fibrositic nodules. Nobody knows what these nodules are and what actually happens at trigger points. Years ago it was thought that they were tiny pieces of fat that had burst through the sleeve of tissue around the muscle. Because they were so tender it was thought that they were due to an inflammation of the fibrous tissue—hence the name fibrositis. However, we now know that this is not the case. Another idea was that the muscle had gone into spasm at that point because of damage to a nerve in the spinal column.

Whatever the reason it is often worth trying an injection into a tender trigger point. As the needle must hit the exact spot that is

tender, the injection process itself can be very painful, but the
patient is (or should be) comforted by the information that if the
injection hurts and, particularly, if it stirs up the actual complaint
itself, it is more likely to be helpful in the long run. If the injection is
painless, the trigger point probably has been missed and a good
result is less likely. Some doctors perform these injections whilst the
patient is asleep under a general anaesthetic in order to spare the
patient the pain of the injection. However, when the patient is
asleep, it is impossible to identify the precise position of the trigger
point and the results are not as good as when the patient is awake.

The injection usually consists of a small quantity of cortisone-
like drug mixed with local anaesthetic. Cortisone-like drugs given
in this way do not carry the same risk of problems or unpleasant
side-effects that may happen if they are taken regularly by mouth,
especially if in a large dose. The local anaesthetic will 'deaden' or
'freeze' the tissues so that within a minute or two the pain of the
injection and of the complaint itself will disappear. However, the
effect of the anaesthetic wears off within three or four hours and the
pain may return. Indeed it may become somewhat worse than
before for a day or so. The real improvement, hopefully, will start
within two or three days and the back pain can clear up completely
in a week or so. Sometimes it only partially gets better and it is
worth trying a second shot.

As we do not know what a trigger point is, it is hardly surprising
that we are equally ignorant about how the injections work. It could
be the anaesthetic, the cortisone, or indeed the needling itself acting
as a type of acupuncture. Nevertheless some patients are very
pleased with the results and as the method is so simple it is often
worth trying.

Epidural injection

The technique of epidural injection is much more complex and used
only for intractable problems when back pain and sciatica have
failed to get better with the types of treatment already mentioned.

Within the spinal column and lining the vertebral canal is a tough
layer of fibre-like tissue known as the dura. The spinal cord and
nerve roots run down the canal inside the dura before they pass out
between the vertebral arches. The epidural space lies outside the
dura between it and the inner margins of the vertebral canal (Fig. 7).

In this form of treatment an injection is given directly into the epidural space.

Only doctors practised in the method use this technique. The epidural space is entered by a long needle inserted directly from behind, or passed upwards from just below the coccyx or tail bone. The injected material consists of a mixture of anaesthetic and a cortisone-like drug. Afterwards the patient will have to rest for at least an hour or two.

When it works, pain relief following this technique is immediate. In some people, however, it only lasts a few hours or days and then the pain comes back. If this happens, it may be worth trying a second epidural injection as this can have a longer-lasting effect.

There has been some controversy about the value of epidural injections with some research studies finding it helpful and other suggesting it does not work. In Australia, there has been a suggestion that epidural injections of cortisone can be harmful but the evidence for this is very controversial. One careful study was performed in Guy's Hospital, London. Of 100 patients, half received an epidural injection and the other had a sham injection. Those given the proper injections obtained greater relief of pain and more often returned to work. The Guy's Hospital doctors believe that this method can be useful for back pain, particularly if there is also sciatica.

Quite how the technique may work is unknown. One suggestion is that the actual volume and pressure of the injected fluid breaks the small adhesions around the nerve roots, so freeing them. Another possibility is that with damage in the back there is some inflammation and swelling. The swollen tissues rub during back movements so causing more inflammation and swelling and the damage never has a chance to heal. Cortisone is so effective in controlling inflammation that the swelling clears, the rubbing stops, and the back pain clears up. Whichever, if either, of these theories is correct, this method of treatment does hold some promise and is currently undergoing further tests.

Facet joint blocks

As pain can be produced by damage to the tiny facet joints between the vertebrae (Fig. 4), the idea arose of blocking the nerves coming from these joints so that pain would no longer be felt. The original idea was developed in Australia and the technique was performed by trying to cut the nerves with a scalpel inserted through a tiny skin incision. The operation was performed without actually seeing the nerves and it is very doubtful whether all the nerves from the facet joints were cut. Recently injections of phenol, which kills the nerves, have been used instead of a surgical incision. Another idea is to insert a needle and heat it with radio-frequency waves to block the nerves. More commonly, however, the facet joints are injected with a cortisone-like drug and anaesthetic under X-ray control.

The results of facet joint blocks have been very mixed. The actual techniques are constantly being improved but it is too soon to know whether the method will be of real value.

Dissolving damaged discs

Enzymes are biological catalysts; chemicals derived from animal or vegetable material which are capable of speeding up various chemical reactions which occur in the body. We use certain types of enzymes in washing powders as they hasten the dissolving of biological tissues and will rapidly remove stains from clothes.

One enzyme, chymopapain, which is obtained from the papaya or pawpaw fruit, is able to dissolve the nucleus of the intervertebral disc. An interesting experiment is to drop some disc material into a solution of chymopapain and watch it disappear over a few hours. On the basis of observations like this, chymopapain was injected into discs in an effort to dissolve them medically rather than remove them at a surgical operation. The technique is called 'chemo-nucleolysis', which means chemical lysis or dissolving of the nucleus. Because chymopapain is such a powerful enzyme, it is essential to be sure the injection is in exactly the right place as otherwise the wrong tissues might be dissolved. The procedure is performed under direct X-ray control to confirm the position of the needle tip in the nucleus before performing the special injection.

The results look very promising and seem to hold up in long-term studies. It is likely that chemo-nucleolysis will become more widely used. Most of us would prefer to be treated by injections than by an operation. However, it is still early days: the technique requires a very high degree of skill and the method is only available in a few very specialized centres and only for certain types of disc problem.

One problem that has emerged is that some people are sensitive or allergic to chymopapain. Sensitization arises following some previous exposure to the chemical. Several centuries ago, the Polynesians at the time of feasts and festivals would wrap cuts of meat in papaya leaves to make them tender and succulent. Papain is an important component of meat tenderizers which are widely used today, particularly in the United States. It helps 'to ameliorate the hardships of an affluent but toothless society'. The reason is that the enzymes will dissolve the tough fibres in the meat so softening it in the same way as chymopapain dissolves discs. Those who eat tenderized meat can become allergic to the chymopapain and then develop reactions following the injection. Skin rashes are the commonest problem. Fortunately, meat tenderizers are used very little in Britain.

Surgery for low back pain

Although back pain is so common and patients are often seen by orthopaedic surgeons, the amount of actual back surgery performed is relatively small. It is the vast size of the back problem rather than the need for operations by individuals that leads to the enormous amount of surgery performed in our hospitals. Although many patients worry about operations for back pain the chances of one being necessary are very low.

To put things in perspective, most attacks of back pain are transient and get better without need of medical help. For every 10 000 bouts of back pain it has been calculated that only 1000 people consult their doctor. Most of these attacks will get better and the general practitioner will only refer about one in seven (140 out of the 1000) to rheumatology or orthopaedic clinics in hospitals for a specialist opinion. Long waiting lists unfortunately are not uncommon in British hospitals, but an interesting benefit from this is that many back sufferers will recover while waiting to see the specialist. One estimate is that about a third get better in this way, so this leaves 100 patients who are actually seen in the clinic. About a quarter of these (25 patients) would require admission to hospital. Most of these 25 patients will either recover with rest, physiotherapy, and medical treatment or will be found to be unsuitable for surgery. Only one in six of these (4 patients) will need an operation. So we are left with a figure of about 4 operations for every 10 000 attacks of back pain.

In the nineteenth century operations on the spine were usually for the correction of deformities. Only relatively recently has surgery for back pain become common. It was the discovery by Mixter and Barr in 1934 that discs can burst and damage nerve roots so producing back pain and sciatica that led to the development of surgical treatment. There was enormous enthusiasm for operations in the early years, in the belief that removal of the damaged disc would cure the problem. More recently this enthusiasm has become tempered by experience and operations are undertaken today only when there are very definite indications. The wrong operation can do more harm than good, so very careful assessment is necessary before taking this step.

First of all the precise cause of the pain must be known. It is no good just opening up the back on spec, and perhaps dealing with one disc, if that is not the cause of the trouble. Surgery is a very precise science and the precision arises because the operation will only affect the exact site at which it is performed. The difficulties in determining the source of back symptoms in many patients have already been discussed. If it is not possible to identify the precise nature of the problem, an operation should be avoided. The spine is so complex that the exact approach adopted by the surgeon is dictated by the actual procedure to be performed. With a burst disc, the exact site of the back pain and sciatica and the findings on physical examination indicate which disc is at the root of the trouble. The clinical diagnosis is usually backed up by specialized X-ray studies, such as radiculography, a CAT scan, or a MRI scan. This information tells the surgeon whether an operation is likely to help and if he decides to proceed, where to make his incision and how to get at the the offending part.

The pain and amount of disability must be severe enough to merit operation. In general, back problems, for which surgery is recommended are not life-threatening although if the nerves to the bladder and bowel are damaged an operation may be required as an emergency. The indications for operation are not absolute but depend on the degree of suffering and interference with normal life. If the pain is so severe as to disturb sleep, is not controlled by adequate pain-relieving tablets, and leads to continued loss of work, then surgery may be advisable.

PLATES

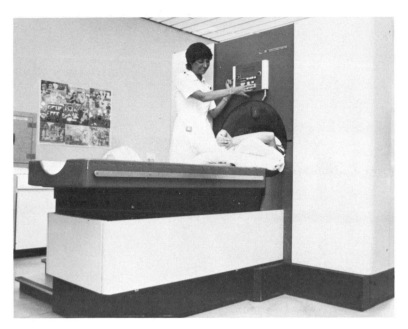

1. Computerized axial tomography (by courtesy of Professor I. Isherwood and Dr. N. Artour)

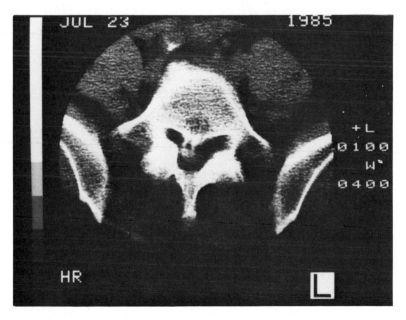

2. CAT scan showing narrowing of the vertebral canal in central stenosis

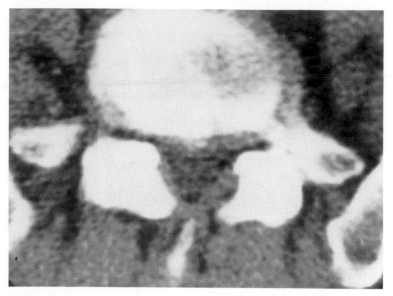

3. CAT scan showing a very narrow intervertebral foramen on the left side in foraminal stenosis

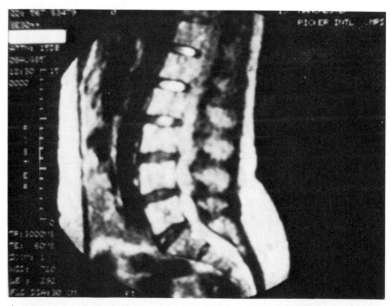

4. Magnetic resonance image of the spine. The upper lumbar discs are normal showing clear differences between the central nucleus pulposus and the outer annulus fibrosus. The lower two lumbar discs are uniformly dark indicating that there are degenerative changes in these discs despite the fact that the conventional X-rays were normal

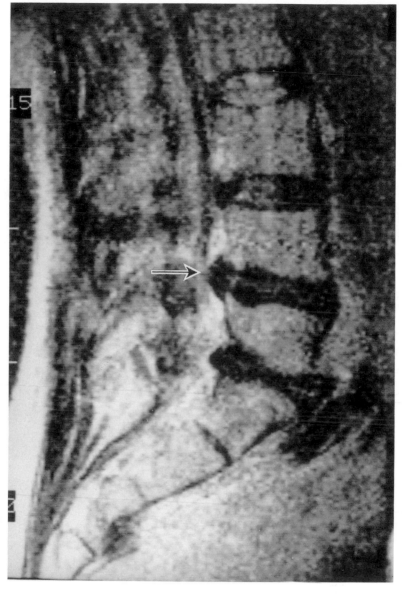

5. MRI scan. There is a bulge at the back of the L$_{45}$ disc (arrowed) indicating a large herniation into the vertebral canal. There is also a small herniation at L$_5$S$_1$

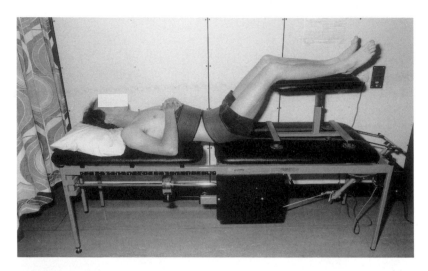

6. Modern traction

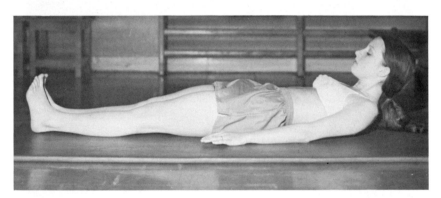

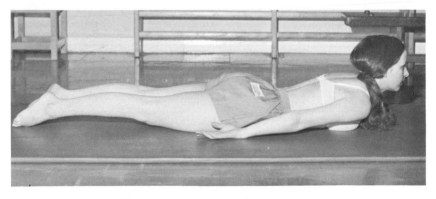

7. Isometric exercises *Upper:* To strengthen the abdominal muscles.
Lower: To strengthen the spinal muscles

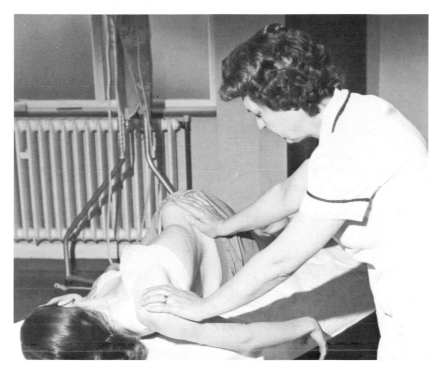

8. Maitland's mobilization of the spine

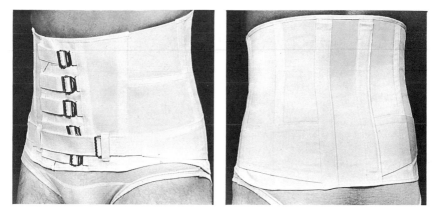

9. A lumbo-sacral corset (by courtesy of Messrs Spencer (Banbury) Ltd)

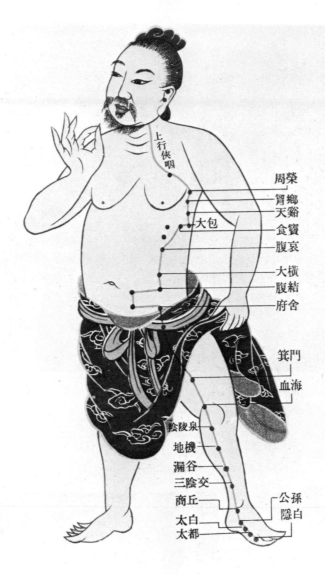

足太陰脾經之圖

凡二十穴
左右共四十穴

上行俠咽

周榮
胷鄉
天谿
食竇
腹哀
大包

大橫
腹結
府舍

箕門

血海

陰陵泉
地機
漏谷
三陰交
商丘
太白
太都

公孫
隱白

圖五十八──仿明版古圖（四）

10. Ancient Chinese acupuncture points (by courtesy of Dr Felix Mann)

11. Modern acupuncture for back pain

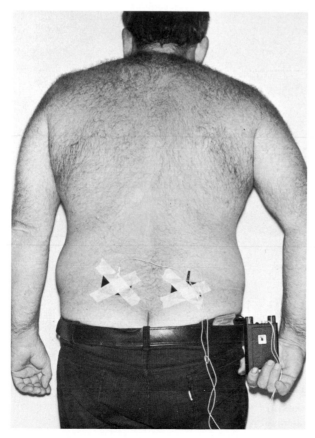

12. Transcutaneous
nerve stimulation

13. A modern range of office chairs designed for back comfort (by courtesy of Hille International Ltd)

14. The automatic Vertebro chair
(by courtesy of Anonima Castelli SPA)

15. The Backfriend Support
(by courtesy of MEDesign)

16. The Balans chair (by courtesy of Neen Pain Management Systems)

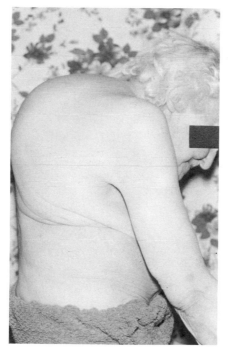

17. A very severe example of osteoporosis

However an operation is not performed as a first line of treatment. An adequate period of simple conservative treatment should be tried first. This may include bed rest, physiotherapy, pain-relieving tablets, and other measures and only if the symptoms persist after an adequate trial should one go on to think about operations. How long is an adequate trial of simple conservative treatment? Again there are no hard and fast rules, but if the pain is no better after three or four weeks then it may be time to consider further measures.

Not everybody is suitable for operation. As surgery is not being undertaken as a life-saving measure, patients with severe heart or chest disease may be unsuitable subjects for a major anaesthetic. Personality problems also come into it. In people who suffer from depression, anxiety, or other psychiatric diseases it may be impossible to separate the back pain resulting from the actual damage in the spine from symptoms exacerbated by psychological factors. In such people the results of operations can be poor and indeed many are made worse. On the other hand in someone with severe, unremitting back pain, depression and anxiety may simply be caused by the persistent nature of the problem and surgery may be the only hope. Very careful assessment is essential before going ahead with surgery under these circumstances.

Finally, the patient must want to have the operation. It is inadvisable to press reluctant patients into having operations. Even with a successful operation there are often some trivial remaining problems and the reluctant patient may well not be satisfied. The wise surgeon will put the pros and cons to patients whom, he thinks he can help but will only operate if the patient is keen to go ahead.

Almost all operations are performed with the patient asleep using a general anaesthetic. The actual operation depends upon the individual problem. For a burst disc, the intervertebral canal is opened up and the damaged disc inspected. It is usually possible to see the burst as a knob of fibrous tissue pressing on the nerve root. The surgeon will remove the whole disc. If only the burst is removed there is immediate relief of the pressure on the nerve root but there is a risk of further recurrence as more material can be squeezed out from the damaged disc.

There have been important changes in the techniques for removing the damaged disc. Sometimes a wide area of bone in the back must be removed in order to obtain access to the whole of the disc and if more than one disc is involved this area may have to be extended up and down the spine. However, surgeons are keen to reduce the amount of bone that must be removed as the removal of a lot of bone can lead to some weakness of the structure of the spine. It may be possible to enter the back between the bones either by direct approach or by microscopic discectomy. For this, a surgeon inserts a small tube to look down using an operating microscope and removes the disc through the tube. A tiny telescope can be inserted into the disc from outside and the disc removed through it. This is known as arthroscopic discectomy. Even lasers are sometimes used to dissolve the disc contents. More recently a technique know as automated percutaneous discectomy has been developed in which a special cutting needle is inserted into the disc. This sucks the disc material into it and then removes it so that only a minute surgical incision is required. The advantages of these newer techniques are a very tiny scar, minimal disturbance to the muscles and tissues of the back and avoiding removal of bone. However the surgeon does not get as good a view of the damaged disc so that sometimes it can be difficult to ensure that all the damaged tissue is removed. These newer techniques are still being developed and evaluated but they do provide hope of making spine surgery much easier in the future.

At the same time as dealing with the disc, the surgeon has to make a decision about whether to fix the two vertebrae together. This is known as spinal fusion. If there is any tendency for a vertebra to slip forwards or backwards then he is likely to perform a spinal fusion. He will also look critically at the size and shape of the spinal canal and intervertebral foramen. The problems of spinal stenosis and the ways of detecting it have been described in Chapter 4. Many patients with back pain and sciatica have smaller canals than normal, so placing them at special risk of damage to the nerve roots. Sometimes this narrowing is not obvious even at operation as the exit canals are located very much to the sides and are quite deeply hidden. Modern scanning is extremely helpful to the surgeon for identifying central or foraminal stenosis. The surgeon looks carefully for such narrowing and if it is found will remove enough bone to create more free space.

Following a straightforward disc removal, most patients start standing and walking within a few days. Often they will wear a lumbar corset for the first few weeks when they start to get going.

They are instructed on the right ways to sit and lift and usually can return to light work within about four to six weeks. In general they are not fit for heavy manual jobs for at least three months and sometimes much longer.

Before undergoing an operation on their back most patients would like a guarantee of success. However, it is never possible to make absolute promises. There is no operation known with a 100 per cent guaranteed success rate. There is always a risk, however remote, of totally unexpected findings, or difficulties apart from the actual problems of the operation itself. However, most patients for whom surgery is advised will be pleased with the results, although there will be a small percentage who are no better or are even worse following this treatment. There are risks attached to any surgical procedure. Even having dental treatment carries some hazard, admittedly minute, but there for all that. Complications of back surgery are very rare and probably occur in no more than 1 per cent of patients.

Most surgeons will put the facts to the patient before performing the operation so that the patient can make up his own mind about whether to have it done. In general, surgery is much better for the sciatic pain felt in the leg than for backache alone. As a rough guide, out of every ten patients, eight are completely relieved of leg pain but only about five or six of back pain. Although these figures do not seem quite as good as one might like, remember that many of these patients have the worst back problems and that other types of treatment have failed.

A decision about surgery requires careful thought by both the surgeon and the patient. However, if the indications are right, the chances of success are very high and the operation is well worth performing.

8

Persistent back pain—arachnoiditis, scarring, and failed surgery

Unfortunately, the back pain problem is not as simple and straightforward as has been described. Many of the different mechanical problems may appear superficially to be similar so that it can be difficult to decide whether one particular abnormality is the source of the symptoms. Most back pains are transient acute episodes but for some patients apparently similar attacks may become long drawn out with the back pain persisting indefinitely. Our current understanding of the back problem frequently fails to explain this enormous variation in severity and persistence and the frustration experienced by some patients is an indication of this. Most patients are very pleased with the results of operations. In a small proportion, however, the operation is not successful and some may actually be made worse. There are many reasons for surgical failure and a precise analysis is required in order to determine why an operation has not worked and what should be done.

The difficulty commonly lies in understanding the significance of changes in X-rays and other imaging tests of the spine. The results of surveys of frequencies of back pain in whole populations performed both in Britain and Jamaica illustrate the problem. The subjects were X-rayed and the severity of the wear and tear changes in the spine were compared with the frequency of back pains. The remarkable finding was that not only was back pain extremely common but also there was little evidence that the wear and tear changes seen on X-ray had much to do with its development. The patients with the worst X-rays did have a higher incidence of back problems than those with normal or virtually normal spines, but the difference in frequency was only about 12 per cent. This means that it is difficult to blame these wear and tear changes as the sole source of back pain for the majority of sufferers and there must be other important factors which are unrecognized, yet play an important part in causing the patients' symptoms.

With the difficulties in recognizing the basis of the problem, psychological factors might be suggested as the cause of the symptoms. Admittedly, depression and anxiety may play an important role for some patients, but this could well be the result of continuing pain and disability for which medical treatment has proved inadequate. A diagnosis of depression and anxiety may be the refuge of the doctor who is diagnostically destitute and is unable to come to any conclusion about the source of the problem. Instead of admitting ignorance he may find it easier to say that it is all psychological, thus placing the responsibility on the patient rather than himself. The statement that pain is of psychological or psychiatric cause should be based on firm psychological evidence and not simply in being unable to pinpoint a demonstrable abnormality in the spine. There may well be important problems occurring within the back that cannot be found by conventional examination and investigation. The concept of pain being either physical or psychological is wrong. The mind and the body interact and we fail to understand any patient's problems unless we appreciate that there may be both damage within the back and perception in the brain which is influenced by emotional factors.

Why does ordinary back pain become chronic?

The majority of back pain problems are acute, unpleasant, but temporary events often related to some mechanical stress. There may be recurrent episodes of back pain which can be related to lifting, twisting, sitting in a poor position, etc. However, for some patients the problems are much more serious. They develop a mechanical back problem similar to those experienced by other people but which fails to get better. They lift, twist, bend, etc. and develop acute backache but despite all the treatments described earlier, their pains persist and may even become worse. They often describe symptoms spreading into both lower limbs, up the spine into the neck, and even into the arms.

In such cases the doctor must re-examine the case and rethink the diagnosis. Is it a mechanical disorder or could it be an inflammatory or other problem as described in later chapters? If mechanical, is there a large burst or some instability in the spine which may require surgery? Is the patient subjecting his back to excessive strains at work or because of a poor posture while standing or sitting or prolonged driving with a poor car seat? Prolonged bed rest and lack of physical fitness can predispose to chronic backache.

Often the back sufferer has been provided with a corset which is worn religiously for several years. The back becomes extremely stiff and it seems as though the corset has added to the problem. Wearing the corset provides a certain amount of relief but the spine stiffens so that any movement is more painful. The result is that the patient wears the corset for longer periods and the back becomes stiffer still and may develop a stuck back (Page 90). The patient finds it very difficult to stop wearing the corset and indeed has become addicted to using the lumbar support.

In other words, the whole case must be reviewed and if the reasons for the chronic back pain are determined then appropriate treatment can be planned.

Failed surgery

The best results from operations occur in the patient with sciatic pain spreading down the leg in whom there is a burst disc which is pressing on the nerve and which can be removed. The results of operations for back-ache alone without sciatic pain are not nearly as good. In some patients the operation works very nicely at first but then the problem will gradually return sometimes months or even years later. In others the operation provides no benefit at all and the pain persists despite the surgery.

What has gone wrong? Why should a patient with a seemingly straightforward back problem not get the hoped for benefit? There are a number of reasons for this, but each case must be considered separately. A very detailed assessment will include a careful review of the previous findings, and clinical examination. Electrical tests of the nerves and muscles, X-rays, and CAT scan or MRI scan will help to show what has gone wrong. This careful analysis is essential. If the patient is going to need another operation on the back then we must be reasonably sure that repeat surgery will help. On the whole the results of a second operation are much less good than for a first operation and for a third or successive operation they can be very poor. Such operations therefore should only be undertaken when there is a very clear problem for which a good result is anticipated.

It is no good operating simply because the patient is in great pain as otherwise they may be worse afterwards.

The original pain may not have been due to a disc problem. The surgeon may have failed to remove the burst disc properly or operated on the wrong disc. All spine surgeons are highly trained and use careful imaging techniques to identify the damaged disc. The chances of failure due to such causes are extremely remote. However, when the pain recurs some time after the operation, it could well be due to further disc material being squeezed out at the operated level or to another disc burst at a different level. We know that people with degenerative changes in one disc have an increased risk of wear and tear changes in other discs so they are more likely to suffer a second disc prolapse. With damage to the discs, wear and tear changes develop in the spinal joints. In particular, this affects the facet joints which may develop degenerative changes and osteoarthritis (Fig. 10) and new bone formation in the intervertebral canal can cause central spinal stenosis (Plate 2) and foraminal stenosis (Plate 3). When a lot of bone is removed there are excessive stresses on the remaining bone, particularly in the back of the spine where small fractures may develop, and sometimes there may be instability with abnormal movements and slipping of the vertebrae on top of one another. In all these problems a very detailed and careful assessment may suggest a further operation but the surgeon will need to be reasonably convinced that this further operation will be successful.

Sometimes excessive scarring can develop around the nerve roots. This can develop following operations or for other reasons. The pain can be very severe and widespread and these patients may suffer the worst of the back problems.

Arachnoiditis and scarring of the nerve root sheaths

Within the vertebral canal (Fig. 4) the nerve roots run down from the spinal cord to emerge through the holes known as the intervertebral foramina between the vertebral arches at each level. The nerves are extremely delicate structures and are protected by layers of membranes so that they are not damaged during the movements of the spine. The innermost layer is known as the pia and is surrounded by the arachnoid which is a fine cobweb-like protective membrane. In turn, around this is a very tough fibrous layer known as the dura (Fig. 4). These layers form a sac which ends at about the level of the junction between the first and second lumbar vertebrae but there are extensions around the individual nerve roots as they leave the dural sac and the nerves are fully protected as they pass out through the various intervertebral foramina. With the bending and twisting of the spine during movements, the nerves are able to glide back and forth and up and down without damage.

There is a condition in which thickening and scarring occurs in and around these sheaths so that the nerves become squashed and damaged and are no longer able to move freely. Analysis shows the severe damage of the nerves and the numbers of properly functioning nerve fibres may be considerably reduced. This scarring can occur within the dural sheath and affect the arachnoid layer and is then known as arachnoiditis. Excessive scarring can also occur outside the dura and is then called peridural fibrosis.

Abnormal scarring and, in particular, arachnoiditis can be extensive and involve a number of nerve roots producing widespread damage. These patients develop some of the worst back problems. There is chronic persistent pain in the back spreading into the legs and often up the spine into the neck and even into the arms. Frequently, patients complain of burning and pins and needles sensations in the legs. Sometimes they get electric shock neuralgic type pains shooting into the limbs. The back is extremely sensitive and even light pressure such as touching or stroking the skin can cause severe pain. Rarely, it can effect the nerves to the bladder or bowel and cause incontinence.

It was originally thought that archnoiditis was caused by infections in the spine. Undoubtedly this happens in some cases. A wide variety of organisms can be responsible and this severe scarring may be the end result of meningitis. The patient develops an episode of infection with meningitis which may be cured but in some cases, particularly if antibiotic treatment was not started early enough, the healing process is accompanied by severe scarring. Tuberculosis inside the spine is one important cause which fortunately is now rare.

However, infections form only a tiny part of the problem. Arachnoiditis can develop following a spinal operation, or at areas where there is severe degenerative change, or even following the investigation known as oil-based myelography in which an oily material was injected into the spine.

A small proportion of patients who have had operations on the spine may do well intially, but some months later may develop a gradual recurrence of pain in the back and lower limbs which becomes more severe and spreads. This may be due to the gradual development of scar tissue which may be arachnoiditis inside the dural sac or excessive fibrosis around the dural sac—peridural fibrosis. A lot of effort has gone into trying to determine the causes of this exececssive fibrosis following spinal surgery and devising methods of preventing its development. It may be due to some bleeding around the nerve roots themselves during the operation, slight tears of the nerve root sheaths, microscopic fragments of surgical gauze or swabs left behind, or even a very mild infection getting in and otherwise passing unrecognized. In order to stop bleeding at operations, surgeons often use special materials known as haemostatic agents and it is possible that they may predispose towards excessive fibrosis. Some surgeons try covering the nerve roots with fatty tissue at operation in order to protect them.

A major cause of arachnoiditis has been the oil-based myleographic dye which was used some years ago for the diagnosis of a burst intervertebral disc. The most common material used in Britain was Myodil and in the United States Pantopaque. They are no longer used because of the risks of producing arachnoiditis. Instead, water-based dyes are used which provide better details of the inside of the spine with only very remote risks of complications.

The oil-based material was injected into the vertebral canal at lumbar puncture and X-rays taken immediately afterwards. If the column of dye was distorted due to a burst disc then the burst could easily be identified. Unfortunately these oily materials are not absorbed easily and can persist within the intervertebral canal sometimes indefinitely. In some cases X-ray of the spine many years after this investigation will show that droplets of this oily material are still present. For this reason some doctors tried to remove the oily dye after taking the X-rays but it was virtually impossible to get it all out. Over the years, in a small proportion of people, this dye can become a source of irritation within the spinal canal and lead to the development of chronic scar tissue formation. The water-base dye now used is absorbed rapidly and following injection into the canal almost all of it disappears within 12 hours, so there is virtually no risk of producing nerve root damage. We even use it to diagnose arachnoiditis as it enables us to see the distortion of the dural sac and the compression of the nerve roots.

These cases are the most extreme examples of arachnoiditis and nerve root sheath fibrosis. Abnormal scarring can occur in response to a variety of other problems and it may not be so easy to recognize. The gross examples described have been called the 'tip of the iceberg' of the total number of cases and there is a vast number of patients with this problem in whom the diagnosis has been missed. In particular, in patients with wear and tear problems in the back—lumbar spondylosis—abnormal scarring can occur. This may be the additional factor occuring as a complication of mechanical damage that is responsible for the development of the back pain and which is not present in patients with apparently similar degrees of wear and tear but no back problem. This could explain the poor correlation between wear and tear change and back pain. It is these patients with secondary scar tissue formation who develop the more severe and persistent problems whereas for others there may simply be an interesting X-ray change of wear and tear which is of no great importance.

Likewise in the patients with narrowing of the spinal canal and spinal stenosis, scar tissue development may be an important factor in causing the development of symptoms. Although the canal is a bit smaller than normal, it may not be small enough to damage the nerve roots without this abnormal scarring which itself has followed the bony narrowing.

It therefore appears that there is a whole field of pathology occurring inside the spine which is difficult to identify except in the grossest of cases and many severe back problems may develop due to this cause and not be recognized. Awareness of the problem by the medical profession is all important. Too easily patients' problems are dismissed as psychological because the severity of symptoms and disability seem out of proportion to findings on conventional examination.

Newer investigations lend hope that this abnormal scarring can be identified. A myelogram, using an injection of a modern water-based dye, is probably the best way of recognizing arachnoiditis but patients who have developed this condition as a result of previous oil-based myelography naturally feel loath to undergo such a procedure. Modern scanning is beginning to enable us to recognize these conditions without the need for an injection into the intervertebral canal. The CAT scan allows us to see scarring around the nerve roots—peridural fibrosis—but not to see the details of the nerve roots within the nerve root sheaths. However, the latest generation of magnetic resonance image scanners provides much more detail and it is now possible to make the diagnosis or arachnoiditis from the appearance of the nerve roots within the dural sac. The thickening of their linings, sticking together of the nerve roots in abnormal positions, and changes in the structure of the nerve roots enable the diagnosis to be made. The information from the scan is sometimes improved by repeating the scan after an injection into the arm of a material concentrated inside the blood vessels. Because scar tissue contains excessive amounts of blood there is a change in the appearances of the scan so that the scar tissue is identified more clearly. We are now beginning to identify a spectrum of pathology within the spine which has previously been missed and understand some of the reasons why back pain may become so widespread, chronic, and severe.

Before deciding on treatment, a very careful detailed examination and assessment is undertaken to confirm that excessive scarring is responsible for the development of the symptoms and there is no other problem which might respond to some different type of treatment.

If excessive scarring is thought to be responsible for the symptoms in the past, surgeons tried dissecting away the scar tissue in order to free the nerve roots and remove the squashing and compression which damaged them. The immediate results of this type of surgery can be quite good and many patients are pleased by the relief of their pain. Unfortunately, the scar tissue can regrow rapidly so that symptoms return and six months to a year later the problem can be as bad or even worse than it was originally. The scar tissue has reformed and it seems that these patients are predisposed towards the redevelopment of the problem. Today few surgeons are keen on operating for excessive scar tissue except under special circumstances as they know that the long term results are likely to be poor. I have seen patients who have had three or even four laminectomies with removal of scar tissue each time but with recurrence of the pain a few months later. It is clear that further surgery is not the answer for this type of back problem and should be avoided.

Research into arachnoiditis

Understanding of arachnoiditis is helped by a pathologist examining the scar tissue with a microscope. Because surgeons are not keen to operate it is difficult to obtain adequate supplies of material. However, in the specimens that are available, it is possible to see deposits of a material known as fibrin which may stick nerve roots together causing adhesions and may block blood vessels so that they can no longer fulfil their normal function of carrying oxygen and food to the nerves and removing waste materials. Later on scarring develops with thick fibrous tissue called collagen covering and squashing the nerve roots.

If we cut ourselves, we bleed, but after a few minutes the bleeding stops. This is because the blood clots, plugging the hole in the damaged blood vessel. In the process of clotting, a circulating substance dissolved in the blood, known as fibrinogen, combines with itself repeatedly to make extremely large molecules called fibrin which are deposited to form the framework of the clot. Fibrin may occur inside blood vessels or in the tissues themselves. Usually, it eventually dissolves away so that the tissue heals and returns to its normal state. This process of dissolving fibrin is called fibrinolysis and is an essential part of the normal process of tissue repair.

Fibrinolysis is performed by enzymes which are biological catalysts, similar to the biological enzymes in our washing powders. Biological enzymes will dissolve the biological dirt that gets into our clothes; in the same way the fibrinolytic enzymes dissolve fibrin deposited in the blood vessels and tissues.

In patients with severe back probems, this enzyme system is not working properly and fibrin may not be removed. This may be the reason why some patients have long term problems. Measurements of the enzyme activity have shown that lack of enzyme function relates to the severity of the back problem and that it improves in those whose pain gets better.

In population surveys performed both in the United States and Scandinavia, it was found that people who smoke are more likely to develop back pain than non-smokers. It seems as though back pain can be a smoking disease much as chronic bronchitis, heart disease, and lung cancer. There is no obvious reason for this association. One suggestion was that the back pain patient could not get any benefit from medical treatment so he smoked in order to get some comfort. Another suggestion was that the smoker coughs more than the non-smoker and that recurrent coughing might damage the back. However, it is known that smoking produces a defect of this fibrinolytic enzyme system in the blood. This predisposes the patient towards this type of damage to blood vessels inside the back, so leading to risk of developing back pain, in the same way as it may be associated with damaged blood vessels in the heart and an increased risk of developing heart attacks.

This enzyme change is only one factor associated with persistent back pain and it could well occur as a result of damage to the blood vessels rather than causing it. There is a substantial number of patients in whom there are other problems. Nevertheless, this enzyme change is common, suggesting that vascular damage plays some part in these cases.

Identification of the enzyme defect suggests that if it could be corrected, fibrin could be removed and the back pain improved. The search is on to find ways of increasing the enzyme activity. Unfortunately there is no easy method. For heart disease, a material known as tissue plasminogen activator or tPA, which stimulates the enzyme activity dramatically, is infused and can be very effective in dissolving blood clots. If given immediately after a heart attack it helps to reopen an obstructed coronary blood vessel and save life. The best results occur when it is used very shortly after the onset of the heart attack; if delayed by more than a few hours it is too late for it to have any real benefit.

tPA is not suitable for chronic back pain patients. It is extremely expensive, must be given by infusion into a vein, and its effect on the enzyme system is short-lived and only makes changes during the period of the infusion itself. It is not a suitable treatment for patients with a long term problem such as chronic back pain.

Alternative drugs all carry problems. The agent stanozolol is a hormone with most of the hormonal effects taken out of it. However, they have not been completely removed and a small proportion of patients who take this drug may develop hormone complications. Fortunately the side effects seem to reverse when the drug is withdrawn but nevertheless make this form of treatment unsuitable for some patients. Its use depends upon demonstration that the fibrinolytic enzyme system is not working properly and careful monitoring during the treatment period is required. The drug has been effective for patients with venous lipodermatosclerosis, that is patients with a continuous swollen and painful leg following a venous thrombosis. They have a defect in the enzyme system and have deposits of fibrin in and around the blood vessels. Treatment with this drug corrects the defect, reduces the amount of fibrin inflammation and fibrosis in the calf, and reduces the patient's pain and disability. Similarly in other conditions in which blood vessels are damaged such as systemic sclerosis or vasculitis, Stanozolol can correct the enzyme defect and improve the blood flow.

Experience in treating back pain patients suggests that Stanozolol can be helpful for less severe types of back problem. For the very severe cases and in particular those following surgery, it seems to be rather disappointing. Overall, patients have not derived significant benefit, although there are some who have improved remarkably. It seems likely that correction of the enzyme defect can only help significantly if undertaken before there is major damage to the tissues in much the same way as in people with a heart attack the coronary blood vessels must be opened up before there has been death of cardiac muscle. Physical exercise can have a remarkable effect in stimulating the fibrinolytic system. We now know that exercise and physical fitness play a very important role in the rehabilitation of chronic back problems. This may work at least in part through its fibrinolytic effects and improving the circulation in the spine. Studies are in progress to elucidate this further.

So there are exciting developments in research and our understanding of chronic back pain. There are new approaches to treatment but nevertheless there is still a long way to go.

Pain due to disturbance of the sympathetic system

Nothing is ever as simple as it seems. So far I have only referred to nerves in terms of the brain, the spinal cord, the nerve roots leaving the spine, and the nerves themselves. Pain has been discussed arising from damaged tissues and mediated through this, the central nervous system.

However, there is another nervous system called the autonomic nervous system which is mainly concerned with the function of the internal tissues of the body—the heart, lungs, bowel, bladder etc., and also the glands in the skin and elsewhere. This autonomic system has two parts—the sympathetic system which mainly seems to prepare the body for violent activity such as increasing the heart rate and raising the blood pressure, and the parasympathetic system which balances its effects.

Over-activity of the sympathetic system can be a cause of severe pain. In some patients with severe damage in the spine it can cause pain in the lower limb, such as a burning pain in the leg. Often there is extreme tenderness in the painful area and even light pressure on the skin can produce agonizing pain. It is all too easy for such complaints to be labelled as 'psychological' for want of recognizing the cause of the problem.

One test which may be helpful is measuring the temperature of the legs. Over-activity of the sympathetic nervous system makes blood vessels constrict and is part of the fight or flight reaction for which the sympathetic nervous system primarily exists. If the sympathetic system nerves are over-active, the constriction of blood vessels will make the skin become cold in that area. A heat photograph can be taken with a special camera to show the area of low temperature.

Why should the sympathetic nervous system get involved? The chain of sympathetic nerve fibres runs along the sides of the vertebral column. These nerves could easily be caught up and irritated when the spine is damaged. However, it is more intriguing than that. The sympathetic system operates in a different way from ordinary nerves. Sometimes damage to a tissue which the nerves supply may lead to overactivity of the nerves and more continued and chronic pain. This is known as a sympathetic dystrophy. We do not understand it but we know that it can cause major problems.

The importance of this diagnosis is that it may suggest alternative types of treatment. If the sympathetic system is over-acting it may be possible to block its effects by drugs, an injection, or even by a surgical operation. So this is another cause of chronic pain which may respond to a completely different approach.

Treatment of persistent back pain

Every patient with severe chronic back pain needs careful and individual assessment. We are all individuals with different backs and different problems. For the patient with severe back pain it is essential to try to diagnose the underlying cause of the pain and why it has not got better. By this stage most patients have received the conventional forms of treatment. Nevertheless, these may not have been used in the best possible way and the whole treatment programme may need to be re-examined.

Are pain relieving drugs being used? If so, which ones? Several different types have been described. Are they being used in the right dose? Are they timed to be most effective when the pain is at its worst? Has the patient received physiotherapy? What types of physiotherapy? Is the patient continuing to practise the exercises? Have they been given ergonomic and postural advice? What about injections? When, where and how have they been given? What operations were performed and why? What have been the short and long term results? With all this information, combined with a careful examination and up to date diagnostic tests, decisions can be made about any specific treatment.

Conventional treatment does not prove adequate for a number of patients with persistent severe problems in the back and in the lower limbs. Many of these patients become depressed and anxious. This may be a natural response to persistent pain and disability but in turn anxiety and depression exacerbate the severity of the pain and disability. A vicious circle has been established which many patients find difficult to break out of. They become chronic invalids, unable to work, and in severe pain. The prospects for such patients have been dramatically improved by recent developments of intensive rehabilitation programmes. These were started in Dallas in the United States and similar programmes are being developed in a number of centres throughout the world.

In recommending this programme to patients, they often tell me that they have had physiotherapy. By this they may mean that they have seen a physiotherapist for half an hour, two or three times a week, and received cold, ultrasound, deep heat, massage, exercises, manipulation, etc. The new rehabilitation programmes are totally different. First, the underlying principle is that the patient must do the work rather than having things done to him. Second, the treatment is extremely intensive, sometimes every day and all day. Third, the programme will involve measurement of the patients abilities to perform various types of activities and movements, setting goals to be achieved and quantifying progress. Lastly, the treatment is not physiotherapy alone but involves analysis of the job, preparation for work, and psychological counselling. In particular, it helps the patient to understand the nature of their pain and disability and to lead a normal life despite it. The pain has not gone but the patient is taught how to prevent it dominating his or her life. The whole process is known as the 'Functional Restoration Programme' and treatment generally takes about three weeks. Thereafter the patient is seen at frequent intervals to check progress, measure the patients' function, and confirm that the goals that have been set are being achieved.

The results of such programmes have been spectacular. It is hard work and only motivated patients will complete the course, but over 80 per cent of these manage to return to their normal working job. Because of the intensity of the treatment programme, only small numbers of patients can be dealt with at any one time. It is labour intensive and as a result very expensive. The resources for this treatment on the British National Health Service are limited at present. However, they are beginning to appear and we hope that they will become more generally available before too long.

9

Prevention of back pain

Back pain affects most of the population sooner or later. There is more work lost in British factories from this cause than from literally any other problem. On the basis of the old adage that prevention is better than cure, much effort has gone into identifying those most likely to suffer from back pain, the types of work likely to cause it, problems with posture at home and at work, and improving methods of undertaking various tasks. Such studies cover all aspects of human life and many of the problems interrelate in complicated ways. It is often difficult to identify the role of any single factor in production of back pain because of the complex associations with related problems. Nevertheless, progress has been made and we are able to provide a considerable amount of advice and recommendations to minimize the back problem. There is still plenty of scope for a more detailed understanding of how man interacts with his environment and develops back pain, for improving the advice that is available, and above all for seeing that his advice is actually put into practice.

Who gets back pain?

Gender seems to influence most aspects of our lives and the incidence of back pain is no exception. In industry, the problem is much more frequent in men than women. However, the explanation of this difference is not at all clear. It could be that the male spine is built differently from the female's and is damaged more easily. It seems more likely, however, that as men on the whole undertake heavier work than women they are more likely to damage their backs. Also, the same backache may allow someone to continue in a light job but not in heavy manual work.

Measurements show that as a crude approximation women possess about 60-70 per cent of the strength of men. This is because women are generally not only smaller but also their bodies contain a higher proportion of fat and lower proportion of muscle. There is a greater incidence of back problems in those performing the heaviest work, who are mainly men, but in light to moderate work groups back problems are of similar frequency in both sexes. There is not much one can do about one's sex but these observations may well be a pointer in indicating the amount of physical activity the spine can stand.

Back problems affect all ages. The greatest incidence in industry occurs in those between 35 and 50 years old with a decline thereafter. This is quite surprising because it would seem likely that the gradual loss in strength occurring with ageing would put older workers at greater risk of back problems. There are several possible explanations. It could be that those with back troubles seek alternative lighter jobs as they get older so that only fit workers remain within heavy industry, or that the younger, less skilled, employees fail to recognize tasks beyond their physical abilities and so more readily injure themselves, whereas the older workers treat such jobs with more respect.

Being overweight is an important risk factor. The excess must be carried by the trunk which is supported by the spine and so in the long run obesity can aggravate back problems. Overweight back sufferers should diet in order to get to their ideal weight. Losing weight is easier said than done. Like smokers, those who are afflicted recognize their problem but have difficulty in doing anything about it. I do not recommend crash diets which involve virtual starvation with a seemingly satisfying loss of weight occurring within the first few weeks. Experience shows that patients will only tolerate a crash diet for a short period of time and sooner or later are unable to stand it any more. They succumb to a craving for food and after a hard struggle eventually regain all they have lost. I recommend a much more gradual loss of weight by adopting a diet that can be lived with for life. By avoiding fats, cakes, sweets, chocolate, and sugar and refusing second helpings it should be possible gradually to slim down. It is important to avoid going hungry by eating regularly but not excessively. Many overweight people join group classes in which they can receive advice and help about their diets and on how to lose weight. These classes are often remarkably successful perhaps because the obese person realizes he is not alone in trying to lose weight and the sense of dieting together will encourage those who would otherwise give up too readily.

The tall members of the population are also somewhat more likely to develop back pain than normal-sized people. This is probably because of the excess leverage they produce when bending forwards. There is nothing one can do about one's height; it simply remains a pointer in suggesting avoidance of excessive bending.

Physical fitness and exercise

'Athletes do not suffer from back problems, therefore exercise is good for your back.' This seems a plausible suggestion, but unfortunately it is not as simple as that. After all if you suffer from backache you could not be a successful athlete. Therefore the observation that athletes do not get backache may simply reflect that back sufferers do not become athletes in the first place.

Of course, athletes do suffer from back problems and all national teams, football clubs, and many other athletic organizations have their own physiotherapists, much of whose work is in helping athletes with their backs.

Regular exercise is good for the back. The two extremes, total laziness or grossly excessive stresses on the spine can both lead to the development of back problems. So the best advice is regular but not excessive exercise combined with general physical fitness. For the healthy, fit, nonback sufferer, the important thing is to keep fit and undertake any regular exercise that is enjoyed. Sport is good for you but one must be careful to avoid excessive lifting and poor positions that put undue stresses on the back. For those who have had back problems exercise should be aimed at strengthening the back and tummy muscles whilst avoiding excessive and sudden twisting and lifting. In particular, sporting activities such as walking, cycling, and swimming are safe whereas those in which there may be sudden unexpected twisting movements such as squash or tennis do carry some risk. It is not easy to avoid sudden twisting movements in these sports when one is playing hard.

Pre-employment medical examination

In an effort to minimize the back problem in industry, many applicants for jobs will face medical checks before they are finally accepted. Employers regard these as particularly important if the work involves heavy manual labour as they hope to avoid placing their workers in the wrong jobs by such means. They may well have a vested interest in trying to avoid paying workers lying in bed with a bad back and particularly in minimizing the risk of compensation claims in case the back pain is blamed on some incident occurring at work. The aim is to identify those most likely to develop back problems by the initial screening examination and either not take them on or give them some less arduous post.

Although such an approach may seem logical, unfortunately the results of pre-employment medical screening have been very disappointing. Other than the factors already mentioned there is little to find by physical examination to indicate likely back sufferers. The examination of the spine or indeed the whole body provides virtually no clues indicating who is at special risk. The only really helpful point is a previous history of back troubles. Someone who has had spinal problems before, and particularly if they have had several attacks of back pain, is likely to suffer further problems, especially if he has to perform heavy manual work. From the points of view of both the worker and the employer it is better that the back sufferer should undertake a job within this physical ability.

In some industries, the pre-employment examination included X-rays of the spine and used these to exclude potential back sufferers. Unfortunately, the relation between X-ray changes and back pain is very poor and if all those who show some abnormality on the X-ray are refused there would be very few left to actually undertake the work. It is very doubtful whether X-rays can be used in this way and studies show little change in the size of the back pain problem with use of this screening technique. In a study in North America there was no difference in the X-rays of groups of workers without back troubles and those disabled by them. This issue is not settled, however. In a study in Minnesota, when the patients with gross X-ray changes were excluded from employment, there was a considerable fall in the incidence of back problems. However, this was at the cost of rejecting about 28 per cent of the applicants purely on these grounds and there must have been many who were refused work but never developed back pain.

In addition, spine X-rays require a high dose of radiation. Although this is necessary for some patients with back problems, it is not acceptable as a mass screening technique, particularly as the results are of such doubtful value.

Back pain and industrial tasks

The alternative to trying to exclude the employee who might develop a bad back is to look at industry, identify the tasks that may produce back problems, and modify them accordingly. Although statistics are not altogether clear, there does seem a greater risk of low back pain for those involved in heavy industry and manual work. Interestingly, the incidence in nurses is equal to that of heavy industry, whereas policemen get off quite lightly. Although nursing might seem a relatively light occupation, it frequently involves considerable back strain in bending over beds and lifting ill patients. Nurses in geriatric wards are at the greatest risk because they commonly have to deal with severely disabled and often confused elderly people who may co-operate poorly while being moved. Unexpected movements may produce sudden strains on the spine and acute back pain. It is hard to believe that being a policeman confers special immunity to back problems; it is more likely that back sufferers leave the police force quite rapidly and only those that are completely fit will remain.

Simply labelling industry as involving 'heavy' or 'light' work is extremely crude and superficial as there are so many different tasks within a single trade. In the coal mines the work varies from work at the coal face to transporting the coal, working the lifts, and even desk jobs in the office. Detailed analyses of individual occupations are more important.

For example, it has become clear that standing still in one spot continuously for hours at a time will lead to aches and pains, particuarly in the back. There is a need to move about regularly and change position. On the other hand, sudden and unexpected movements are liable to damage the back and produce back pain. In a survey of over 3000 individuals, low back pain was much more frequent in those who often had to perform sudden physical efforts than in those who rarely or never did so. Sudden twisting movements are particularly bad in this respect.

Because of the risks of heavy manual work, measurements have been made of the physical forces required for various jobs and comparing these with suggested maximum limits. The problem with legal limits on the maximum physical effort required in a job is that the way the task is performed can be as important as the load itself. Moreover, there is the implication that any effort within the prescribed limit is harmless. Repeated lifts of lesser weight may be equally damaging. Authorities who wish to play safe may set the limit so low that virtually no work can be done. The International Labour Office has suggested limits for weight-lifting in industry but there is no agreement about whether their figures have a valid basis. However, they did find that those involved in very heavy work had a three-fold increase in incidence of back, knee, and shoulder problems, a five-fold increase in hip problems, and a ten-fold increase in elbow problems. In Britain detailed proposals and regulations for workers handling heavy loads are currently under consideration. These include the need to consider the size and nature of the load, the working conditions, and the personal limitations of individuals. Recommendations towards reducing hazards to those involved in manual handling include the better design of handling systems, matching particular tasks to individuals, and careful observance of properly taught manual handling practices.

Although limitation of loads alone will provide only a crude guide because of so many other factors, it is helpful to have some indication of what is acceptable. The following guidelines are under consideration:

Level	Actions
Below 16 kg (35 lb)	No special action required, provided those relatively few individuals likely to face serious risks when handling weights of this order have been identified.
From 16 kg (35 lb) to 34 kg (75 lb)	Administrative procedures required to identify those individuals unable to handle such weights regularly without unacceptable risk, unless mechanical assistance is provided.
From 34 kg (75 lb) to 55 kg (120 lb)	Unless the regular handling of weights of these magnitudes is limited to effectively supervised, selected, and trained individuals, mechanical handling systems should be employed.

Level	Actions
Above 55 kg (120 lb)	Mechanical handling systems should always be considered at this level. Where not reasonably practicable, selective recruitment and special training are essential, since even with effective supervision very few people can regularly handle weights of this order with safety.

Simply measuring the weight to be lifted is a very crude way of determining the stress and risks for the back and takes little account of the circumstances and postures in which the effort is performed or the shape of the object being handled. For example, we all know how much more effort is required to hold a weight at arms length than close to the body. The reason is because the twisting force produced on the shoulder joint is a combination of the weight of the object and the distance away from the shoulder. This is the same phenomenon as occurs in a child's swing in which the heavy weight of father on the one side close to the centre of the swing can be counter-balanced by his child on the other side sitting much further away from the centre. The way to protect the back is to hold objects close to the chest and not at arms length.

Equal care must be taken with objects that have to be lifted high up above shoulder height and even more so above head height. Balance becomes extremely difficult particularly if the object is heavy. Slips and strains occur easily and sudden movements readily lead to pain.

Careful positioning before making any lift is essential. The best way to lift a compact load is between the knees and use the powerful hip and thigh muscles. This is far easier than raising it above waist height which relies on the weaker shoulder and elbow muslces.

A new and interesting approach developed in Michigan involves comparison of the maximum force involved in the particular lift with the maximum that could be achieved by very strong workers in that identical posture. This provides a lift strength rating (LSR) which is defined as:

$$LSR = \frac{\text{maximum load lifted}}{\text{the predicted maximum lift capability}}$$

When the job required an LSR of 0.2 or greater, there was a considerable increase in the incidence of low back pain. The research provided charts showing the maximum strengths of large strong men in various positions and the physical forces required in particular tasks are compared with these. If the LSR is 0.2 or more then the job is altered to make it easier. This method provides a real advance in understanding the physical requirements of various types of manual labour and more widespread application should lead to the elimination of hazardous tasks and their replacement by more acceptable procedures.

However, the LSR test can only be applied to about 70 per cent of manual jobs. In the remaining 30 per cent the lifts do not readily fall into the patterns described because they are performed with one hand and unevenly and perhaps performed on moving objects. This method is being developed further.

This and other similar tests are exciting approaches to the problem of back pain in industry. They point the way to determining jobs liable to cause back pain, developing better methods of performing the same task, and ensuring that individual employees are not asked to exceed their physical abilities.

Back pain is common in industry. Whether the work actually causes the pain or simply brings on the problems in a person with a weak back is often not very clear. Whichever is true, there are many workers who continue in unsuitable employment despite considerable back problems. The failure to change jobs or modify the working posture can be due to a number of factors. Amongst these are lack of good advice, inflexibility of working patterns, loyalty to comrades or employers, lack of alternative work, and financial constraints, as with labourers recommended for other less physically demanding but also less well-paid jobs. A better understanding of the relationship between work practices and stress on the back should reduce the magnitude of the back problem in the future.

Standing

Prolonged standing at work and at home should be avoided. However, such advice often is not practical. Many jobs require the worker to be on his feet for much of the day. Back problems can be minimized by standing in the right way. Frequent changes of position are important and there must be room to move about and to stretch at frequent intervals. As far as possible the head should be kept up with the shoulders straight and the hollow in the low back preserved. Not only is this the most comfortable position but also it looks the most attractive. The slouch looks bad and also leads to overstretching of the ligaments of the spine and backache. High heeled shoes tip the pelvis forward and make one try to arch the lumbar area backwards to compensate. In turn the patient slouches forward in the back of the chest (Fig. 15). The resulting posture produces a lot of strain in the spine. Although high heeled shoes may be fashionable, they should be avoided for prolonged use, particularly of back sufferers.

Industry often requires its employees to undertake bench work. Standing and leaning over a bench with the back bent and insufficient room for the legs is a very effective method of producing backache. The height of the bench should allow the employee to work in the upright position. The right height to work is level with the elbow when the arm is hanging freely by the side of the body. The work surface should be about 8 cm (3 in) below this. Below the bench there must be room for the feet, and the most comfortable position is with one foot in front of the other in order to assist balance (Fig. 16).

Lifting techniques

Practices to avoid are lifting objects above eye level, carrying heavy items at arms' length, which magnifies the effect of the weight, trying to lift badly shaped objects, and pulling and pushing at low levels. Careful thought and redesign of the task should reduce these problems.

Lifting is probably the most common single cause of episodes of acute back pain. Apart from limiting the weight of the load, much research has gone into improving techniques of manual handling and lifting with training programmes now given in many industries (Fig. 17).

The most common way of lifting is the freestyle technique and is used by people who have received no instruction on how to lift. The knees are straight or slightly bent and the back is rounded. The spine is unsupported by the muscles and the ligaments are readily over stretched. The freestyle lift of heavy objects is a potent cause of back problems. Until quite recently the straight back/bent knees method was regarded as the method of choice. The lifter crouches down in front of the object with the back straight, grasps the object, and then lifts upright using the hip and thigh muscles. Despite initial

Fig. 15 Good (*left*) and poor standing postures

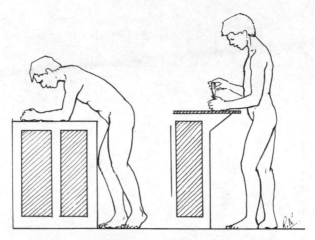

Fig. 16 The right and wrong *(left)* ways to work at a bench

enthusiasm considerable doubts have crept in about this method. The feet are close together producing a small base and an unstable starting position for the lift. The full flexion of the hips and knees needed to lift a heavy object from the floor causes the heels to rise so that only the front of the foot remains in contact with the floor. This makes the base smaller and the position even more unstable. The result is that the lifter must concentrate on maintaining balance as well as the lift itself. It is this iniitial phase of raising the object off the floor which has led to the current doubts about the straight back/bent knees technique.

Following a great deal of thought and much practical experience, the kinetic lift method is believed to be the optimum way of lifting and is now taught in many industries. The principles of the technique involve keeping the back straight although not necessarily upright, the chin in, the right positions of the feet, a good grip on the object with the arms close to the body, and using the body weight to assist in moving the object. The method is taught in the factory by a demonstrator. He would usually start by explaining the back problems, the risks caused by faulty techniques, and the likely benefits from better handling methods. He obtains the respect of his audience by demonstrating how to move a heavy, awkward object such as a large oil drum and illustrates common faults such as poor grip, the freestyle lift, and the effects of a poor foot position and follows this by teaching them the kinetic method applied to the various types of problem that the workers are likely to meet.

The first step is to size up the job and think whether or not the object is too heavy or bulky. If so, the task should be divided into two or more parts, another colleague should be asked to help, or a mechanical means of lifting should be used. The position of the feet

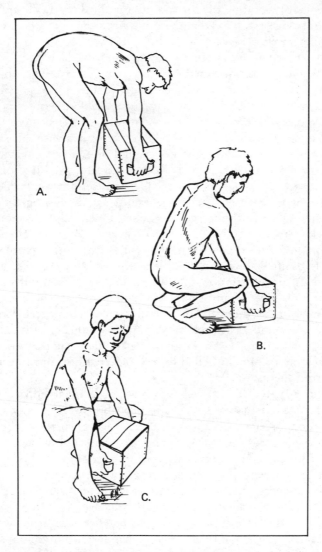

Fig. 17 Methods of lifting. A. Freestyle. B. The straight back/bent knees method. C. The recommended kinetic technique

is all-important. They should be spread about 50 cm (20 in) apart with one foot behind the object and the other by the side of the object and pointing in the direction in which it is to be moved. This has two benefits. The broad base is very stable and avoids balancing problems. By pointing the forward foot in the direction of travel, it will not be necessary to twist the spine when the object is lifted but simply to move the rear foot. The worker squats down with the hips, knees, and ankles flexed and the chin in. The back is kept straight and usually inclined forward as necessary. The object is positioned between the knees and as close to the body as possible. A good grip is essential and if not readily available the object should be tilted onto one corner and gripped firmly at a free bottom corner on the opposite side. The grip should be performed with the palm of the hand and the roots of the fingers and thumb and not with the fingers alone as they are much weaker. Finally, the lift should be performed with the leg muscles. The load is set down by repeating these steps in reverse. The worker must avoid twisting the back throughout the lift, the carry, and the set-down. The load should be held close to the body (Fig. 18) or even over the back always keeping the spine straight. A heavy load at arms length particularly if it is to be lifted above the shoulders, often leads to trouble.

Practical demonstration of lifting techniques are reinforced in industry by safety campaigns and wall posters. There is good evidence from studies in various industries of considerable reductions in the numbers of back injuries by use of this kinetic handling technique. In those factories adopting the best handling methods the back injury rate has fallen by up to 50 per cent illustrating the potential benefits.

Unfortunately, this advice has failed to make much impact on the back problem as a whole. This is probably because only a tiny proportion of the working population are properly taught the kinetic method of lifting. The number of qualified instructors is very small. Appreciation of the benefits of this handling method should lead to rapidly expanding training programmes.

There are improvements in the design of containers. The primary purpose of a container is to protect whatever is inside. Today, thought is also given to how it will be handled. If it is to be lifted then its size, shape, and total weight are important. Ergonomists are designing improvements in the type and position of handles and grips and even the texture of the surface.

Seating

Chairs should be designed for comfort. However, some of the worst back problems arise in those who have to sit all day, particularly at work. Commonly, problems are caused by poorly-

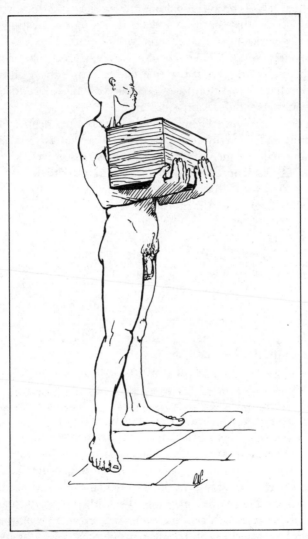

Fig. 18 Upright posture with load

designed chairs and would be prevented by better seating. Much research has been devoted to improving the design of chairs but most has been directed at chairs used in offices rather than for domestic purposes. This is probably because the costs involved in developing and manufacturing well-designed products put them out of the reach of the average domestic purchaser. Also, one might cynically think that back problems due to poor seating make workers less efficient so that it actually saves money to spend more on the purchase of better chairs. Nevertheless, the principles established in the design of better office furniture apply equally to chairs purchased for the home and many domestic products now incorporate current ideas about design.

The good chair will feel comfortable if it provides proper support to the body and a healthy sitting posture. If a chair is the wrong size or shape it will be uncomfortable. For this reason chair designers look to measurements of the human frame in order to determine the dimensions of their chairs. However, they do not make a chair specifically designed for the mythical average man as so few of us are actually of that size. Rather, they choose dimensions that will fit a large proportion, usually 90 per cent, of the population. Sometimes this is by having adjustments available on the chair or on other occasions simply by allowing a certain amount of leeway. A chair that would exactly fit the human body would not be tolerable for more than relatively short periods. We all change our posture regularly and frequently during any sitting period. If there is too much control, only a single position could be adopted and this would rapidly produce fatigue. A definition of good chair is 'one which permits as many good postures being adopted as possible without interference with the work'.

When sitting, the weight of the trunk is taken mainly by the ischial tuberosities which are the twin bones within the buttocks which can be felt when sitting on hard surface. They are specially adapted for this purpose and it is normal that they take most of the weight when sitting rather than the surrounding softer and more sensitive tissues. The skin over the two ischial tuberosities is thicker than that covering the rest of the body, with the exception of the soles of the feet, which also have to carry a lot of weight. If the material of a seat is too soft then the pressure is not borne by these bones but spread out over the whole of the buttocks compressing the skin, muscle, nerves, and blood vessels and this can cause numbness, tingling, and loss of feeling. This is why a seat that is too soft is uncomfortable. A seat exactly contoured to the shape of the buttocks would also be uncomfortable as the weight of the body would be borne by these soft tissues. The seat should be fairly flat with a small amount of upholstery but be firm so that the pressure is concentrated around these bones. It is for this reason that canvas seats are uncomfortable. Their reputation as 'numb bum' seats is due to the spreading of the load widely over the soft tisses.

To compensate for the firmness of the seat, in office chairs springing is often provided in the centre column. This may have a mechanism such as a gas cylinder which can absorb sudden shocks when sitting down and prevent the jarring which would otherwise occur. Such a mechanism also allows for adjustment of the height of the seat. The material in which the seat is upholstered should be porous to avoid the sweating which develops with impermeable materials.

The height of the seat should allow the user to place the soles of his shoes on the floor in comfort. There should be no pressure on the backs of the thighs with the feet resting squarely on the floor. If the seat is too high blood vessels and nerves become pinched resulting in numbness, tingling, and extreme discomfort. The recommended measurements are that the seat height should be slightly less than the height of the underside of the thigh in the sitting position. A seat that is low can also cause problems. The hips and knees will be excessively flexed and the sitter will not be able to maintain the normal hollowing of the lower back. He may be forced to adopt a posture involving bending forwards and this commonly produces back problems.

The depth of the seat should be about 16–21 cm (6–8 in) less than the distance from the back of the buttocks to behind the knee. If the seat is too long it will press on the back of the calf and produce discomfort. The person will be forced to slide forwards to relieve this pressure and will lose the benefit of the back-rest. Seats for use in crowded places and for very short periods may be very shallow. They should be deep enough so that the twin bones, the ischial tuberosities, can rest upon them. If shorter than this no support will be provided.

Most seats are perfectly horizontal. This is the most useful position although a slight backward slope will allow full use of the back-rest. The width of the chair seems less important. Usually they are made wide enough for the broadest person likely to use them to sit in comfort.

When sitting on a stool, the muscles of the back, particularly in the lumbar region, will contract in order to maintain the upright posture. Indeed they are probably more active in this position than when standing. Such continuous muscle activity is tiring. In the absence of a back-rest, the weight of the trunk may be taken by leaning forward and resting with the arms on a table or by slumping the trunk into the round back position. The strain is born by the ligaments of the spine and this can produce back pain.

A back-rest must be strong enough to support the trunk and yet allow movement of the spinal column and of the arms. It does not have to be rigid. A stiff sprung support can be extremely comfortable. The aim of the back-rest is to provide a relaxed position with support of the spine in the lumbar region. With a correctly designed lumbar-rest, support higher up is unnecessary. The high backs found in some executive chairs are imposing but do not have an important function. The back-rest should provide support in the lumbar region below the level of the shoulder blades. If it is too high when the subject relaxes, the lumbar muscles slump and the subject sits with the low back bent forwards—a potent cause of back problems. If the back-rest is too low it will come into contact with the sacrum or tail bone and push the occupant of the chair forward on the seat. The lower edge of the lumbar support must therefore clear the sacral region. In typists' chairs, the position of the support is adjustable.

The optimum angle of slope of the back-rest of the chair depends on the purpose of the seat. The alert position for a secretary is more upright than the comfort position of her boss. Some chairs will have a tilt mechanism so that the occupant can relax lying backwards in the chair. The mechanism must be sprung so that it does not tilt back too easily.

Arm-rests are far from necessary. If present, however, they should be at the right height. They should be at the level of the elbow when sitting. If lower than this they will not provide adequate support to the elbows and if higher they merely get in the way. The latest designs of office chairs incorporate these ideas and various dimensions can be adjusted for individual comfort. For example, a range of British chairs has been created specifically to minimize back problems, and has power-assisted adjustments of both the angle of the back and of the seat height (Plate 13). There is an Italian range which automatically adjusts to provide optimum support with change in position of the body. When leaning forwards, for example at a desk in order to study documents closely, the seat and back-rest shift forwards automatically, and when relaxing backwards the seat moves forwards but the back-rest tilts backwards (Plate 14).

The same principles apply when choosing an upright chair for use in the home. The height, depth of the seat, amount of cushioning, and provision of a lumbar support are equally relevant. For the back sufferer an upright chair of this type may be the answer as low easy chairs can be extremely uncomfortable. When buying a chair for home use, pay particular attention to the various points mentioned. Above all, sit in it for a few minutes to see how comfortable it is. Most chairs do not feel too bad when sat in for only a moment or two. One should only be satisfied with the chair if it is still comfortable after more prolonged testing.

Unfortunately, the same enthusiasm for the development of office chairs has not gone into the design of armchairs and other easy chairs. Many of these have cushioning that is far too soft and without lumbar support so that the back adopts a rounded position and sooner or later starts to ache. The best chairs are well upholstered with a firm seat. This is tilted backwards so that the user leans against a back-rest in which there is a lumbar support at the appropriate height. A high back can support the head when lying back in the armchair and is of more value than in an upright chair. It must not push the head or the back of the chest forward compared to the low back. This would be almost guaranteed to produce backache.

In past years, cars were notorious for poor seating and people whose jobs depended on a lot of driving, such as sales representatives, would develop dreadful back problems as a result. Back pain due to prolonged sitting in a poor posture induced by car seats is a well-recognized hazard of that profession. Fortunately, today we hardly see the bench seats or the hammock shaped seats which had particular reputations for producing back problems.

Ideally the driver's seat should be designed separately from that of his front seat passenger, but this does not happen in practice. Proper support is required for the driver who is in a working

position, whereas a relaxed position is ideal for his accompanying
passenger. The driving seat itself should have a firm surface with a
slight backward tilt and the back-rest contain a lumbar support at
the right height. In some cars the amount of lumbar support is
adjustable. The back-rest may also be shaped to provide some
lateral support so that the driver is not affected by sidesway.
Temporary back-rests are available if the car seat is uncomfortable
but a well designed car seat is much better.

In an effort to make chairs and car seats more comfortable
temporary back supports are often used. The idea is to provide
some support in the low back and help maintain the lumbar
lordosis. For some people a small pillow or cushion may suffice but
there are specially designed back supports available some of which
seem particularly helpful providing that the support is in the right
place. The design of these supports is crucial. Many prove
satisfactory as they provide lumbar support in the wrong area or
they readily slip out of place. The lumbar roll is one of the most
useful devices. It consists of a simple padded tube which is carried
about and can be slipped behind the back as needed. There is an
interesting new device called the 'Back Sling'. This consists of a
supporting belt around the lumbar region with straps around the
knees which pulls the back forwards and provides lumbar support.

Plate 15 shows one design of back support in which a lot of care
and thought has gone into the exact shape and strengthening to give
maximal anatomical support in the critical lumbar area of the spine.
This particular model also has a detachable seat designed for
maximum comfort and the angle between the back-rest and the seat
can be adjusted.

Because of the unsatisfactory nature of many chairs and the desire
to try to improve seating and prevent back problems arising,
furniture designers in Norway have developed a new and original
type of chair (Plate 15). The principle is that the seat is tipped
forwards and the weight of the body is supported by the knees. As a
result the normal curvature in the lumbar area is preserved and the
stress on the back considerably reduced. This position is much the
same as that in which children sit naturally. They lean back on their
heels with a straight back and relaxed stomach muscles. It was from
observations of children that the designs of these chairs for adults
were developed. Since the original design was produced, the range
of chairs has been expanded enormously. Many back sufferers find

these chairs helpful. However, they are still very new and only time will tell about their long-term values.

Much thought has gone into designs of seating for other special purposes. In aircraft the seating must allow for relatively tight packing of the passengers, room to get in and out, and scope for reclining as well as many of the other points already mentioned. The pilot must not only be in a position of comfort for a long flight but also able easily to grasp a number of controls and read a myriad of instruments.

Tables and desks

The design of seating should not be considered in isolation from the desk, table, or bench at which the occupant is working. A table that is too high or too low will produce stresses on the spine and contribute towards back problems. In the office, the chair and desk should be considered as a single unit so that the proper relationships are maintained (Fig. 19). For clerical work, the desk surface should be at about the level of the elbows when sitting upright, and the arms hanging down. This means that the forearm will be horizontal when writing. A higher desk produces a cramped position and the edge of the desk will press on the forearms. The shoulders will often be raised to bring the elbows and forearms onto the desk and the muscle activity will lead to fatigue. For physical work performed sitting at the bench the worker's elbows should bear the same relation to the work surface as if he were doing the same job standing upright.

The vertical distance between the undersurface of the table and the floor and any foot-rest must allow adequate clearance for the knee and thigh. There should be enough room to allow the occupant to cross his legs with a gap between the chair seat and the undersurface of the table of about 25–30 cm (10–12 in).

Conclusions

It is clear that mechanical factors both cause and aggravate the back problem. Much of this develops during work. Improving physical fitness, regular exercise, an understanding of the physical requirements of various jobs and capabilities of employees, coupled with limitation of excessive physical activity, instruction on appropriate

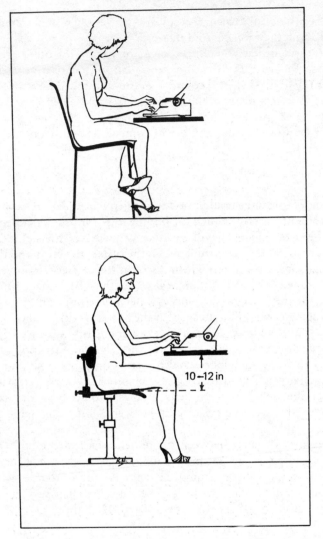

Fig. 19 A poor posture (*above*) and the ideal position for a typist at her desk

manual handling techniques, modification of the work environment and provision of chairs which help to provide good posture for the back should prevent much of the disability we meet today.

10

Ankylosing spondylitis and related disorders

In this book so far the major emphasis has been on the mechanical problems occurring in the back and how they can be prevented and treated. However, backache may develop for other reasons. Recognition of alternative causes of the problem is always important and that is why the back sufferer would always seek medical advice, particularly when the pain develops for the first time.

Inflammation may occur in the joints of the back. There are a number of possible causes of inflammation but most frequently it is due to the condition known as ankylosing spondylitis. This name is developed from 'ankylosis' which means a stiffening, 'spondyl' which refers to the spine, and 'itis' which is the medical suffix indicating inflammation. In other words it is an inflammatory condition of the spine which may lead to stiffening. An ankylosing spondylitis-like problem can occur in other diseases such as ulcerative colitis, Crohn's disease, psoriasis, Reiter's disease, and some other disorders. Initially these back problems were regarded as separate disorders with similar features but recent advances in the study of how ankylosing spondylitis is inherited indicate a close relationship between them. In particular ankylosing spondylitis may appear in one patient and another disorder such as psoriasis or Crohn's disease in a relative. Each of these disorders can be complicated in an individual patient by features of the others, including not only inflammation of the spine but also other problems. Today these conditions are grouped together as the 'seronegative spondarthritides' which means that the serum in the blood when tested is negative for the rheumatoid factor found in rheumatoid arthritis, and that they involve inflammation of the joints of the spine. This group of disorders is quite separate from rheumatoid arthritis although years ago ankylosing spondylitis was regarded by some specialists as rheumatoid arthritis of the spine.

This view is no longer held although true rheumatoid arthritis can, on occasions, affect the back as well as the joints in the limbs.

Ankylosing spondylitis

In its severe form this condition is easily recognized. There is complete loss of the movements in the joints of the back so that the spine becomes completely rigid. The worst cases are as stiff as a poker so the condition is sometimes known as 'poker back'. However, unlike a poker the posture is not upright. The ankylosing spondylitic often ends up in a characteristic but unfortunate position: intensely round-shouldered with a stoop or kyphosis of the upper part of the back. The patient will stretch his neck backwards in an effort to keep looking forwards and avoid looking at the ground. With proper and early treatment it is usually possible to avoid this long-term picture. That is why the disease should be diagnosed as early as possible and the appropriate treatment programme instituted.

Ankylosing spondylitis has been around for a very long time. The changes can be recognized by examination of skeletons so that archaeological evidence is readily obtained. In the excavations of the Egyptian mummies in the Valley of the Kings there is evidence that a condition rather like ankylosing spondylitis existed thousands of years before Christ. In the fifth century AD Caelius Aurelianus described a patient who was 'afflicted with pain in the nates, moved slowly, and could only bend or stand erect with difficulty'. The Bishop of Cork in the eighteenth century described a man who was completely rigid from his feet to his head. He had a job as a watchman in a sentry box because he could only look in one direction. A nineteenth-century medical book illustrates a case with such severe deformity that the head was pointing not only downwards but also backwards so the patient could only look behind him between his legs. Fortunately, such disasters do not occur today. Even now, however, we see people who have developed rigid spines and poor postures in past years. Once the joints have set, it is difficult to do anything the problem. With modern treatment most of the long-term stiffness and deformities can be prevented.

The condition most often appears in young men. It usually begins between the ages of 15 and 25 years but can start at both younger and older ages. In any young man with backache the question of ankylosing spondylitis must always be considered first as it is remarkably frequent in this age group. One of the easiest ways to find cases is to enquire about backache in groups of university students or army recruits. The disease is thought to occur about five to ten times as frequently in men than women. Cases do occur in women and they can develop severe disease. Being female does not exclude a diagnosis of ankylosing spondylitis although it does make it less likely.

There has been slight reticence in quoting the frequency of this condition because we now believe that mild forms are very much more common that previously appreciated. Many backache sufferers have a sub-clinical type of ankylosing spondylitis and the diagnosis may be missed for years if not indefinitely. The condition may affect 2 per cent of the whole population which means that in Britain there would be well over a million sufferers. These mild forms occur in equal frequencies in the two sexes in contrast to the male preponderance already cited.

Why is it then that the obvious disease appears so much more common in men? The explanation is far from clear. Possible reasons are (a) that the disease is rather worse in men than women; (b) that men on the whole undertake heavier work than women and so have more problems at work; (c) that men complain more than women; (d) that when the back pain occurs in women it is treated as relatively unimportant and probably due to gynaecological problems in contrast with the 'proper' back pain that men suffer! Whatever the reason for this peculiar conundrum, we now realize that mild ankylosing spondylitis is common in both sexes, and a frequent cause of backache, although more severe problems are less frequent in women and predominantly occur in men.

The inflammation usually starts in the sacro-iliac joints, the pair of joints connecting the sacrum to the pelvis; it gradually spreads up the spine to involve first the lumbar area, then the back of the chest and the neck. Sometimes there is also inflammation in the hips, knees, or feet. The inflammation may affect the lining of the joints but has an important characteristic separating it from rheumatoid arthritis and other types of joint disease. This is the involvement of the attachment of ligaments to bone. Inflammation starts there and heals by forming a tiny knob of new bone. The ligament is still attached to the tip of this knob and further inflammation gives rise to progressive lengthening of the bony protuberance, so eventually the whole ligament may be converted into bone. The end-result is that the joints can no longer move and it is this process that eventually will produce the rigid poker spine. The same type of inflammation can happen to ligaments elsewhere and particularly below and behind the heel where spurs of bone may form.

The initial symptom is of low back stiffness and pain. In the early stages the former predominates with an aching quality which only becomes a proper pain as it gets worse. The symptoms are aggravated by rest and relieved by exercise. It is very characteristic that the patient is wakened in the morning by aching and stiffness in the back. He tosses and turns in bed but eventually is forced to get up and obtain relief by doing a few physical jerks. This may happen in the early hours much to the distress of the patient (and his wife) who are unable to get a good night's sleep.

This pattern of symptoms is described in the Bible. Job was a wealthy merchant whose faith in God was tested by the infliction of all sorts of problems. Amongst these Job describes how 'wearisome nights are appointed to me. When I lie down, I say, when shall I rise and the night be gone? And I am full of tossing to and fro until the dawning of the day . . . and the days of affliction have taken hold upon me. My bones are pierced in me and in the night season, and my sinews take no rest.' Clearly he had ankylosing spondylitis.

At this early stage of the disease the back may feel and look normal during the day although some backache may return when the patient is tired. This pattern is in complete contrast with the mechanical types of back pain described earlier in this book in which the pain is made easier by rest and worse following physical exertion. The spondylitic also finds that stiffness and aching returns if he sits still for any long period and he finds it better to get up and move about frequently.

In mild ankylosing spondylitis, the movements of the back are preserved, especially by the time the patient is seen by a doctor in the surgery when the early morning stiffness will have worn off. It is only later that more severe stiffness persists throughout the day and examination shows restriction of back movements in all directions including bending forwards, backwards, sideways and twisting. The normal hollowing in the low back may become lost so the lumbar area appears flat. The spine in the back of the chest is normally curved slightly forwards and this becomes worse so that a stoop develops. At the same time the neck feels stiff and painful and movements are restricted.

As the stiffening spreads though the back the patient experiences increasing difficulty in bending or twisting. If he wishes to look behind he is forced to turn his whole body rather than his head alone. Backing the car can be extremely difficult and in severe cases the driver must rely on mirrors rather than look behind. Eventually the back may become completely solid with no movement possible. One saving grace as this happens is that the pain disappears. Pain occurs only when damaged joints move so that a completely solid spine will be painless. However, the disability will persist.

Rarely, patients develop progressive stiffening of the back without much in the way of symptoms. They may develop a completely solid spine without realizing that anything is wrong. This has happened in army officers who are trained to stand bolt upright and get struck in that particular position without realizing it.

The same type of inflammation occurs elsewhere. When the joints connecting the ribs to the spine are involved, their movements are lost with reduction in chest expansion. Fortunately, we breathe with our diaphragm as well as the rib cage. Otherwise the spondylitic would have difficulty breathing properly. Inflammation can also affect the joints in the lower limbs, and most often the hips. Progressive reduction in hip movement alone produces problems, but when the spine is stiff as well the combination can rapidly lead to total disability. Providing the lower limbs are unaffected, a stiff back does not interfere with one's ability to walk. Even with stiff hips it is possible to walk about by swinging the trunk. When both hips and back are stiff, however, getting out of a chair and walking about may be impossible. Fortunately this combination is rare. Inflammation may also occur behind the heel at the attachment of the Achilles tendon or under the heel producing 'plantar fasciitis'. There is pain and swelling interfering with walking and making it difficult to find comfortable shoes.

The diagnosis of ankylosing spondylitis is confirmed by an X-ray. The initial changes are found in the two sacro-iliac joints. However in early disease the changes are very subtle and the joints may appear quite normal so that the X-ray cannot be used to exclude the diagnosis. Later, features of ankylosing spondylitis are found in the rest of the spine and indicate the severity of the condition.

The bone scan is a particularly useful test for diagnosing early ankylosing spondylitis. A minute dose of radioactive substance is injected and concentrates in the inflamed tissue. A photograph is taken with a Gamma camera which shows where this material is to be found and excessive amounts in the sacro-iliac joints indicate the cause of the problem. This test is frequently positive when ordinary X-rays do no show features of ankylosing spondylitis so it allows the physician to make the diagnosis before serious damage to the joints of the back has developed.

Inflammation can develop in other tissues of the body and sometimes precedes the onset of back pain. In the eye the iris, which surrounds the pupil, may become acutely inflamed, so that the eye feels painful and vision becomes blurred. This develops in about a third of patients with ankylosing spondylitis. Those who develop one attack are likely to suffer a recurrence, and repeated bouts if not properly treated can permanently damage the iris and lens and interefere with eyesight. Inflammation may also occur in the intestines. These types of chronic inflammation of the bowel are known as ulcerative colitis and Crohn's disease. Careful study of the bowel troubles in spondylitic patients does show that a significant proportion have these problems. Either the back or the bowel troubles may start first so it is not possible to say that one complicates the other but rather that they are associated. Very rarely inflammation may also affect the heart. It may damage the aortic valve, the function of which is to ensure that blood leaves the heart in the right direction to pass round the body. The damaged valve may leak, so interfering with the work of the heart. If necessary, this valve can be replaced at operation by a heart surgeon.

Treatment

With proper treatment it should be possible to prevent most of the long-term problems of ankylosing spondylitis. However, the responsibility for this largely lies with the patient himself. The fundamentals of the treatment programme are constant attention to posture to prevent deformities arising and regular physiotherapy and exercise to stop the joints becoming stiff and losing their range of movements. The physiotherapy treatment must be done every day and if possible twice a day for at least a quarter of an hour each time. Although this does not sound much it is remarkable how few patients adhere to it. Hours are spent in the pub or watching the television yet excuses are found for never having time for these exercises. Undoubtedly, repetitive exercises may seem boring but this is small price to pay in the fight against deformity and disability. It is not possible to emphasize enough the importance attached to these two patient responsibilities—attention to posture and physiotherapy.

Attention to posture means constantly stopping oneself from slouching forward but sitting and standing upright in order to correct this tendency. The tall elegant African girls who balance water jugs on their heads and at the other extreme the girls in finishing schools who are taught deportment by walking with books on their heads both stand in the right way. This is the posture that must be preserved. The slouch becomes fixed only too readily.

The exercise regime will usually be taught by the physiotherapist in the first instance. However, it is not necessary to be treated by a physiotherapist every day but simply to follow the instructions once they are understood. The exercise programme is aimed at maintaining all the movements of the back and neck including bending forwards, backwards, and sideways, and twisting to both sides. Breathing exercises are included to prevent the restriction of the rib cage. There are exercises for the hips and shoulders and other joints. When performed conscientiously, it is usually possible to prevent most if not all the stiffness that otherwise would develop.

Swimming is an excellent exercise and should be encouraged. The breast-stroke is particularly good for the shoulders and hips, the crawl for the spine and chest, and the backstroke for all muscle groups. However, ankylosing spondylitics should not perform high diving because of the risks of damaging the neck. Other non-competitive sports should be encouraged but care should be taken in those contact sports in which injury may result. It is easy to damage the inflamed back and in advanced disease the spine, although rigid, is weak and fractures occur readily.

When sitting in a chair there should be a proper support in the lumbar region. The bed should be firm and not sag as described in Chapter 5.

Drugs are very effective in relieving the symptoms, particularly in early disease. However, if used alone they will let the patient slouch and develop spine stiffness and deformities in comfort but do nothing to prevent the development of disability. The spondylitic must appreciate that the treatment does not come from a bottle of tablets. Instead he should use medicines to allow him to perform the

Fig. 20. The upright posture and the slouch of the ankylosing spondylitic

exercises more thoroughly. The tablets used are both pain relievers and also control inflammation. Aspirin, indomethacin, the propionic acid derivatives such as ibuprofen, naproxen, diclofenac, ketoprofen, and the other non-steroidal anti-inflammatory drugs mentioned in Chapter 6 are all used. If anything, they are better at relieving symptoms in this condition than in the mechanical types of back pain. This is because the inflammatory element is so predominant here. As the symptoms are at their worst in the early morning, it is usually helpful to time the medicines to be most effective then. This usually means taking the drug last thing before going to sleep. Sometimes they pass through the body so quickly that they lose their effect by the early morning. This can be dealt with by using slow-release preparations in which the active constituent is released over a long period into the intestine for absorption or long-lasting drugs which only pass slowly through the body. Some of these slow-release and long-acting drugs can work for a full 24 hours. If the anti-inflammatory drugs are inadequate and do not properly control the pain, their effects can be topped up with a simple analgesic such as paracetamol.

In former years, deep X-ray irradiation was used as a form of treatment. It was effective in relieving the immediate problems but in the long run made no difference to the patient's progress. Those who received this treatment carry a slightly increased risk of certain complications so that today radiotherapy is reserved for the most difficult cases. However, it is helpful in dealing with persistent area of inflammation outside the spine, such as the heel. Most often, injections of small amounts of cortisone are used for these very localized tender areas. They are particularly effective for pain beneath and behind the heel. Usually the cortisone is mixed with some local anaesthetic so that the injection itself should not be too distressing.

Surgery has only a very small part to play. When there is a severe deformity of the spine, correction by taking out a small wedge of bone is possible and can be remarkably successful. However, it is quite a formidable procedure and not undertaken lightly. Replacement of severely damaged hip joints is now almost a routine operation in many orthopaedic departments. This operation, developed by Sir John Charnley in Wrightington, has revolutionized

the treatment of hip disease in general and can be very effective for
the spondylitic with hip problems.

Ulcerative colitis and Crohn's disease and the spine

In both of these conditions there is persistent inflammation of the
intestines and both may be complicated by back problems and
arthritis in the limb joints. To explain the difference between
ulcerative colitis and Crohn's disease, it is necessary to understand
the functions of the different parts of the bowels. Food, when
swallowed, passes into the stomach where it is mixed up with
various digestive juices and then passed into the small intestine
where the nutritional parts are absorbed. The remaining debris
passes into the large intestine from where it is excreted via the anus
or back passage. In ulcerative colitis there is inflammation of the
large intestine only, whereas Crohn's disease can affect either or
both the small and large intestines. The details of the type of
inflammation differ between the two conditions. However, both
produce recurrent and unpleasant diarrhoea, weight loss, and
general ill health.

The inflammation of the back involves the sacro-iliac joints and
the rest of the spine in the same way as ankylosing spondylitis. If a
patient with ulcerative colitis or Crohn's disease gets backache then
this diagnosis should be suspected. Although the bowel and back
inflammation can occur together their relationship is not very clear.
The bowel disease may be very mild and the back inflammation
severe and vice versa. Either may occur first. On occasion the link
may not be direct with the bowel and back disorders occurring in
the same patient, but instead they occur separately in close relatives.
One has bowel problems and the other ankylosing spondylitis. So it
seems that the association depends principally on inherited genetic
factors making the two run together rather than one being a direct
complication of the other. A particular inherited tissue type, HLA
B27, predisposes towards ankylosing spondylitis. If a patient with
bowel inflamma-tion has this tissue type then his chances of
developing spondylitis will be greatly increased. Recent studies have
shown that certain types of bacterial infection of the intestine, quite
different from ulcerative colitis and Crohn's disease, can also be
associated with spondylitis in genetically susceptible individuals.

If the back pain is due to spondylitis, then the treatment is the same as in the straightforward condition. However, patients with chronic diarrhoea may have difficulty with the suppositories mentioned and prefer taking these drugs by mouth.

Psoriasis and the back

Psoriasis is a very common persistent skin condition which produces a characteristic rash. There are patches of red thickened skin which if scratched gently will produce a myriad of tiny silver flakes. The rash usually develops over the backs of the elbows, the knees, and the scalp. However, it may occur anywhere on the trunk and in severe cases may involve the whole body. Even the skin in apparently unaffected areas shows changes on microscopic examination and the cells are multiplying at a far greater rate than normal. The effects of psoriasis often last for many years although modern treatment usually keeps it under excellent control.

Like inflammatory bowel disease, psoriasis may be associated with disease of the spine and also arthritis in the limb joints. The back problem affects the sacro-iliac joints and the spine in just the same way as ankylosing spondylitis. There is stiffness, low back pain, and progressive development of a stoop and loss of movement and in severe cases permanent deformities of the spondylitic type. Again, inheritied factors play an important role in determining whether spondylitis develops. Those psoriatics who are born with the particular tissue type are at special risk of this complication. The treatment of spondylitis in a psoriatic patient is exactly the same as described earlier for ankylosing spondylitis alone.

Reiter's disease

This disorder is named after Hans Reiter, who described in 1916 the illness in a Prussian cavalry officer serving in the Balkans. He developed arthritis following a discharge from the penis and inflammation of the eyes. As with many illnesses named after an individual, the honour of the name seems arbitrary and unfair because the true credit belongs to Sir Benjamin Brodie, an Englishman, who described the disease in 1818. The correct name should be Brodie's disease.

In this country, Reiter's disease most often occurs as a form of venereal disease, particularly in those who are sexually promiscuous. However, this is not always true and in some it develops following infective diarrhoea; outbreaks have been described in closed communities on ships following a form of food poisoning. In certain cases there is no obvious precipitating cause.

Because this pattern of arthritis and back trouble may arise due to several different causes and also because the connotation of promiscuity is frequently attached to the term Reiter's disease, this type of disorder is often called Reactive Arthritis. In other words it has developed as a reaction to an infection which may be venereal but also may occur following bowel infection. The new name for venereal Reiter's disease is Sexually Acquired Reactive Arthritis or SARA. Similarly we use the name Enteric Acquired Reactive Arthritis when the reactive arthritis follows the bowel infection.

The disease usually starts in young and adult men but younger and older men and women are not exempt. The first symptom is burning pain on passing urine and the desire to do this much more frequently than normal, although the actual volume passed my be very small. The sensation may waken the patient several times during the night in order to provide relief. A discharge from the penis is common and often seen on first getting out of bed. The patient should be referred to a special venereal disease clinic as various types of infection can cause these symptoms and it is important that the right treatment is instituted before any damage is done. For example, antibiotics are required for gonorrhoea and syphilis. In Reiter's disease a swab taken from the penis for culture is often sterile. This is called non-specific urethritis or NSU. A week or two later inflammation develops in the eyes and then in the joints. The arthritis usually starts in the feet and knees but sometimes elsewhere. There may be ulcers on the penis or inside the mouth, a rash on the soles of the feet and the rest of the body and other problems.

The back usually is not affected in the first bout of Reiter's disease. However, these patients often develop recurrent attacks without any obvious precipitating cause, and in subsequent bouts the disease may involve the sacro-iliac joints and the spine in the same way as in ankylosing spondylitis. The symptoms of back pain, the limitations of movement and the deformity are all very similar. Those patients who develop back problems commonly have the same inheritance factor as the spondylitic, illustrating the links between these conditions. Moreover, the rash is very similar to that of psoriasis described earlier.

The treatment of the back problem in Reiter's disease is the same as that of ankylosing spondylitis but in addition in early disease antibiotics are usually prescribed for the NSU. The other features mentioned may also required treatment.

The interrelationships of these conditions

Although these various diseases are described separately it is clear that there is a common strand running through them in that they are all associated with similar types of spine involvement. They have an important link with an inherited tissue type. We are all familiar with the typing of red blood cells into A, B, AB, and O groups which is necessary for patients about to have a blood transfusion. Using blood of the wrong group can provoke severe reactions. The white cells in the blood can be typed in a similar fashion and these are known as the human lymphocyte antigens or HLA antigens. Knowledge of these is important for matching donor and recipients when transplants of organs such as the kidney or heart are considered. Accurate matching is essential to avoid rejection.

One of these tissue types is known as HLA B27. In 1973 workers in the Westminster Hospital in London and the University of California in Los Angeles in the United States simultaneously discovered that this tissue type is present in only about 8 per cent of the general population but in 95 per cent of those patients with ankylosing spondylitis. This is the inherited factor predisposing towards ankylosing spondylitis. If you are born with tissue type HLA B27 the risk of developing ankylosing spondylitis is increased about 600 times. In Reiter's syndrome there is the same very close association with HLA B27. The patients with psoriasis, ulcerative colitis, and Crohn's disease who develop ankylosing spondylitis also have a very considerable increase in the incidence of this tissue type.

The reason why inflammation of the spine would be associated with a particular blood cell type is unknown and open to much speculation. One suggestion is that the inheritance gene for spondylitis is located next to that for HLA B27 so that the two tend to be inherited by the same individual. The receptors that determine white blood cell type are located on the surface of the cells. The HLA B27 receptor is structurally very similar to that of certain bacteria. This might mean that the body does not recognize these bacteria as invasive organisms and therefore fails to eliminate them, so they can settle in the spine and produce inflammation. It is still early days to know the answer to this problem.

This inflammatory group of back disorders provides an interesting contrast to the mechanical problems described earlier in this book. It is essential to diagnose them properly because the treatment is totally different from that of mechanical back pain. A number of different conditions were originally recognized under this heading but we are now beginning to understand the complex and fascinating interrelations which they have with each other.

11

Some other back problems

The preceding chapters have covered the more common back problems. However, a number of other disorders may be responsible for back pain. Some can lead to severe damage of the spine if left untreated. They are described in this chapter in order to emphasize the need for skilled medical advice in elucidating back problems. This is particularly important when the pain develops for the first time and if it does not repeat a pattern which has occurred before.

Infections in the back

Infections are due to germs which are usually bacteria or viruses. Bacteria are minute single-celled living organisms that can invade and multiply in the tissues. An infection in the skin produces inflammation and if pus is formed it becomes an abscess. Occasionally bacterial infections occur in the bones of the spine causing osteomyelitis, and if pus develops a spinal abscess forms. The infection has usually spread to the back from elsewhere in the body, such as a boil in the skin. Back pain gradually develops and becomes extremely severe. The patient feels ill and develops a high temperature and often shivering attacks. This is quite different from the types of backache previously mentioned. The treatment involves identifying the particular bacteria and treating it with the right antibiotic. Occasionally a surgeon may drain the pus from spinal abscess.

Tuberculosis is another example of infection. It usually occurs in the lungs. Bone tuberculosis is usually due to drinking milk from infected cattle. In the back the disease is known as 'Pott's disease' after Sir Percival Pott (1713–88). In the past tuberculosis of the spine was a dreaded complication because the infection could severely damage the bones and nerves. With pasteurization of milk and testing of cattle, tuberculosis of the spine is now relatively rare although surprisingly there has been some increase in frequency in the last few years. Modern treatment is remarkably effective in dealing with this condition but it should be started as soon as possible to limit spinal damage.

Another type of bacterial infection affecting the back is brucellosis or undulant fever. This infection is transmitted in milk from infected cows and currently there is an extensive campaign to eliminate brucellosis from dairy herds. Unfortunately, this is not as easy as the elimination of tuberculosis and there is a small risk for those who drink unpasteurized milk from cows that are not brucellosis-free. Veterinary surgeons are at particular risk of developing this infection because of their close contact with cattle.

Viruses do not affect the bones but one virus, that of shingles or herpes zoster, can affect the lumbar nerve roots. Pain develops both in the back and in the lower limbs in the area supplied by the nerve and for several days the problem can resemble mechanical types of back pain and sciatica. However, after a week or so the virus produces a rash in the area supplied by the particular nerve root and this gives the correct diagnosis.

Rheumatoid arthritis and the back

Rheumatoid arthritis is a persistent inflammation of joints, principally in the limbs, which may eventually produce permanent damage and deformities. The diagnosis is usually obvious in more severe cases.

Occasionally the disease affects the spine and occurs in both the neck and the lumbar areas. When back pain occurs in rheumatoid patients it is often difficult to know whether it arises because of the mechanical problems that are described earlier or to rheumatoid involvement of the joints of the back. Until quite recently it was thought that the disease did not affect the lumbar area but this was mainly because of the difficulties in identifying rheumatoid changes on X-rays of the lower back. With modern techniques we now believe that this is much more common than previously thought. The treatment is the same as for rheumatoid arthritis elsewhere.

Diseases of the bone

Bone is not a uniform strengthening material like a steel strut but has a complicated structure. It consists of a dense outer sheath enclosing a meshwork of tough fibres. These fibres are made of tissue somewhat similar to that of the ligaments but strengthened by crystals of a mineral called calcium hydroxyapatite, which are packed into the fibres like tiny bricks (Fig. 21). The calcium in

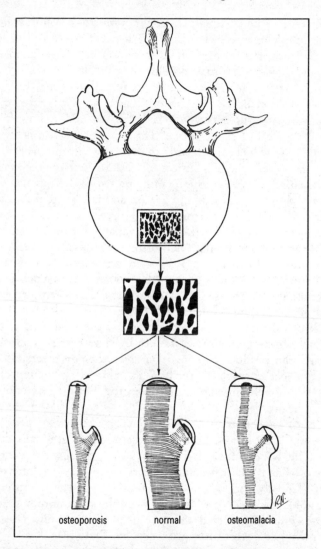

Fig. 21 The structure of the bone of the spine and the changes in osteoporosis and osteomalacia

bones comes from our food and is absorbed from the intestine, provided there is sufficient vitamin D. Both calcium and vitamin D come from dairy products such as milk, butter, and eggs, but vitamin D is also formed directly in the skin by exposure to sunlight.

If there is an inadequate fibrous framework, only a limited amount of calcium can be laid down. The bone is very weak and this is known as osteoporosis. It is common in older people and particularly women. It may develop as a result of certain diseases and taking cortisone and similar drugs for a long time. In another disorder, osteomalacia, the fibrous framework may be formed normally but insufficient calcium is laid down so that the soft tissue is not changed into proper bone. The principal reason is a lack of vitamin D in the diet, particularly in those who live in overcrowded slum areas where there is little sunlight. In Britain, osteomalacia most often affects Asian immigrants but also is seen in the elderly who rarely go out of doors and live on an inadequate diet. Lack of calcium can be due to a chemical called phytic acid which combines with calcium in the food making it unavailable for the bones. Phytic acid is present in bread but fortunately is destroyed during fermentation. However, it persists in unleavened bread such as chapatis and may be partly responsible for the osteomalacia in Asian immigrants. A recent trial of chapati-free diets led to a significant improvement in the calcium in their bones.

Lack of calcium and vitamin D can be due to disorders of the intestines. In certain diseases failure to absorb food constituents normally can produce osteomalacia and other disorders. In some this is due to a sensitivity of the bowel to gluten, a protein present in wheat. Simply eliminating gluten from the diet may be enough to control the problem.

In both osteoporosis and osteomalacia there is progressive weakening of the bones. In the spine a stoop may gradually develop because the bone in the vertebrae gives way, causing frequent small fractures. Each time a fracture occurs there may be intense pain which gradually gets better over a few days as the fracture heals. These are known as 'crush' fractures and the sufferer may gradually become round-shouldered and lose height as a result. This is the reason why old people often grow shorter (Plate 17).

An acute attack of pain in the back is probably due to a small fracture. During the painful period the sufferer rests in bed giving the fracture a chance to heal. He is able to get up after a few days; the rest should not be too long as immobility itself can weaken the bone further. Of course weakness of the bones can also affect the arms or legs. Old people are liable to falls and break their hip or wrist. This is usually due to osteoporosis. The sort of fall that young people tolerate with no problem is often enough to produce a fracture in an elderly person. Careful testing is needed to find out why the bone has become weak and in particular to distinguish osteoporosis and osteomalacia. If a specific cause can be found then appropriate treatment is given.

We know that prevention of osteoporosis is easier than cure. A good diet with plenty of dairy products containing calcium and vitamin D together with regular exercise help to preserve the strength of the skeleton. Osteoporosis most often develops in women and the major cause is reduction in the sex hormones which occurs after the change in life. In particular, women who have had a hysterectomy and removal of the ovaries are at additional risk and measurements show that the strength of the skeleton is depleted over the years in such cases. Hormone replacement therapy (HRT) is in vogue for many reasons but a particularly important one is its role in preserving and improving the strength of the bones. HRT is probably the most effective way of doing this and there is a very strong argument for giving it to all patients following hysterectomy and removal of the ovaries, particularly if performed at a young age. If the womb is not removed, HRT must be given in monthly cyclical course and include both oestrogen and progesterone. Unfortunately it can bring back periods, a most unwelcome reminder of youth for these women. On the other hand, if the patient has had the uterus removed then only oestrogen is necessary and it can be given as patches stuck onto the skin rather than by tablets.

Alternatives to HRT are available and are still being developed. Sodium fluoride and calcitonin are sometimes used. However a very important development is the use of drugs known as phosphonates. One of these, etidronate does work. It is only taken for a few days each month or even for about ten days every three months with calcium tablets taken on the non-etidronate days. It had the advantage of not being a hormone. However, it does not help any of the post-menopausal problems other than the weakness in the bones.

Paget's disease

In this condition there is excessive formation and turnover of bone.
It was described by Sir James Paget who lived from 1814 to 1899.
The disease occurs in all countries but with enormous variations in
frequency and there is now a strong suggestion that it is caused by a
virus infection in the bone. One common site for Paget's disease is
the bones of the back. Normally, in the adult, once formed, the
bone usually is replaced extremely slowly with only a very small
amount of bone being removed and reformed. However, in this
disease there is a dramatic increase in both the removal and
formation of bone. The result is that the bones become enlarged,
deformed and painful. Until the last few years little could be done
other than provide simple pain relieving tablets which failed to
control the actual Paget's disease itself.

The first drug that was effective in actually controlling the Paget's
disease was calcitonin. This is a hormone present in all of us and
formed by the parathyroid glands in the neck. It acts to increase
deposition in and decrease the removal of calcium from bone so that
the bone becomes stronger and less liable to damage. The usual
forms of calcitonin in clinical use are derived from either salmon or
porcine parathyroid glands. These are satisfactory for most patients
but some become allergic to these substances. Very recently, by
tissue culture, it has become possible to manufacture calcitonin that
is identical to the human product. This seems much safer and less
liable to produce allergic reactions and may well in the long run
replace the salmon and porcine versions. A disadvantage of
calcitonin is that it has to be given by injection usually three times a
week. This can be a great nuisance for many patients particularly if
elderly or disabled.

A more recent development are substances known as biphosphonates. Amazingly these substances are important constituents of
many of our washing powders! However, I do not advise anyone to
start eating washing powder for Paget's disease. There are a number
of different types of biphosphonates and one, etidronate, is now in
widespread clinical use. Other improved biphosphonates are
probably on their way. The biphosphonate may be taken in tablet
form by mouth with the obvious appeal of that sort of treatment. It
can be very effective for certain types of Paget's disease but care

must be taken over the dose as, in some circumstances, it can lead to weakening of the bone.

A new biphosphonate still in the trial stage is APD. It is given as an infusion into a vein. The results of this treatment can be excellent with some patients developing remissions lasting many months. However, it is early days and research on this compound is still being carried out.

Tumours in the spine

Fortunately these tumours are rare. A spinal tumour may be a primary growth or secondary to disease in other organs. The tumour may be benign which means that is does not spread, grows very slowly, and if removed, will not recur. However, it can also be due to a malignant cancer or, occasionally, to leukaemia and Hodgkin's disease. A spinal tumour causes pain in the back. If the nerve roots are damaged there may be weakness and loss of sensation in the legs or the lower part of the body. Careful examination and tests are needed to make the right diagnosis. Treatment with medicines, surgery, or X-rays may be required and can be remarkably effective.

Back pain in pregnancy

The mechanical weight of the baby in the womb alters the centre of gravity of the mother's body. The ligaments of the pelvis are looser than usual so that the normal lumbar hollowing increases, causing strains on the ligaments of the spine. Low back pain is common. The joints of the pelvis separate just before birth to allow the baby to pass through safely during delivery. As a result the sacro-iliac joints may become tender and painful.

The best advice to the mother is to have adequate periods of rest in a properly supported bed, to avoid putting on too much weight, and to wear a pelvic support. The vast majority of back pains of this type recover completely following delivery but on occasions the loose sacro-illiac joints do not close completely and persistent pain results. A firm pelvic binder is usually all that is required.

Referred pain

When pain is felt in the back it has not necessarily originated there.
This concept has been discussed previously: pain can be felt in the
leg due to a burst disc in the spine. Equally, disorders within the
abdomen and pelvis can be felt in the back. In particular peptic
ulcers, inflammation of the pancreas, and various types of gynaecological disorders can produce back pain. Generally, there are
features of the problem to indicate their source. Examination of the
abdomen or pelvis will reveal tender areas and pressure will produce
back pain. With gynaecological problems the pain is often related to
the time of the periods. Moreover, the back itself is not tender and
movements do not exacerbate the symptoms.

12

Social, psychological, and psychiatric aspects of back pain

Of all the difficulties in dealing with back pain, these aspects present perhaps the greatest and most challenging problems. The interaction of organic disease and behaviour is difficult to understand, even for straightforward medical problems where the actual physical cause is known. In patients suffering from back pain, we often do not know whether it all arises because of disorders in the back, whether it is entirely a psychological problem, or whether the two interact in some complex fashion. Nevertheless, the patient's pain is every bit as painful whether it is due to organic disease in the spine or develops entirely in the mind. There is a great tendency to think that psychogenic pain is imaginary and not real, in contrast to pain due to a physical illness that requires treatment. All pain is felt in the mind, however it is caused. If anything, the pain associated with psychological and psychiatric disturbances can be worse than that of organic disease alone. A sympathetic and proper understanding of the nature of the problem can lead to a constructive plan of treatment.

We all react in different ways to adversity. Some will tolerate unpleasant events with little emotional reaction while others suffer considerably. These differing psychological reactions occur in the back pain patient and an essential part of the clinical assessment is to determine the role of the mind in the interpretation of individual symptoms.

Malingering and compensation neurosis

Perhaps the simplest problem is that of the malingerer—the person who deliberately pretends he has pain in order to avoid something unpleasant or else to obtain some benefit. Obvious examples are children who complain of a tummy-ache or back pain in order to avoid going to school, or a worker who wants a day off in order to watch a football match. No amount of treatment to the back could make any difference here. Although this type of malingering does occur, it is probably far less common than newspapers would have us believe. It is easy to exaggerate the importance of this problem. It may account for the odd day off but deliberate pretence of back pain by and large does not cause persistent disability.

Doubt is often thrown on the veracity of a patient's statement about back pain if the symptoms follow an accident and there is to be legal action to obtain compensation. One often hears both doctors and lawyers say that such patients will fail to get better until they have received their compensation, and that once the settlement is achieved the pain will disappear without treatment. This is called a compensation neurosis. The symptoms are either fabricated or develop subconsciously because of the financial benefit to be obtained. A diagnosis of compensation neurosis is often invoked in such patients when there are no definite clinical findings to explain the symptoms. There is suspicion on the part of the doctor that he finds difficult to conceal. The patient attempts to convince the sceptical physician and may exaggerate his symptoms, so making the diagnosis and treatment more difficult. The end-result is mutual distrust and persistence of the problem.

Although these views about compensation neurosis are held so widely, there is little evidence in their support. In an Australian series of accident victims who injured their backs, those who had their claim settled still had continuing problems, although not quite as bad as in those involved in continuing litigation. A study of a similar problem of persistent headache after head injury failed to find any effect of compensation on the outcome. Another Australian study showed that after apparently similar injuries, back pain patients who were seeking some form of compensation had more severe pain and disability than others for whom no claim was possible. It is true that following a back injury the persistent pain can be due to a combination of the actual damage and psychological factors, but to simplify the problem as just being 'after the money' is a gross misrepresentation of the position. It can impugn the motives of patients when no justification exists. There may be damage in the spine not demonstrable by routine tests which could explain all the problems. Moreover, the psychological reactions of normal people following an accident can be just as much an injury as an actual fracture or laceration. If the shock produces an anxiety state or depression this should be considered in the same way as physical damage. Legal minds try to disentangle the actual effects of the accident from the patient's previous conditon. If someone already has backache and becomes a bit worse after an accident, his compensation will be very different from that awarded to someone with a previously normal back. A weakness in the back, putting it at greater risk, would also be taken into account. Likewise, his previous mental state may well influence the psychological reactions to the accident and may play a crucial part in deciding the outcome. A person who is prone to psychological problems, has an accident, and develops back pain thought to be of psychological origin, is likely to receive less compensation than a person whose disability can be blamed on the accident alone.

The effects of accidents, legal claims, and compensation on back pain are worthy of further research.

Psychological aspects of back pain

Some people suffer from pain in the absence of or with minimal disease to account for it. A simplistic view used to be that people born with a particular personality or meeting particular types of problem might develop certain patterns of symptoms. Although there is some truth in this, modern psychological studies indicate a very complex interplay between medical, psychological, and social factors in the development of the patient's response to disease.

Psychological factors are a combination of the patient's inherent personality and experience during development, particularly childhood. Perhaps the most obvious example of personality influences are those people who have the condition known as alexithymia which means 'without words for feelings'. These people are unable to experience emotional states, particularly if adverse, such as anxiety or anger. Instead, these emotions may be translated into and felt as physical symptoms such as back pain. Alexithymia may be due to a physical abnormality in the brain such as lack of the nerve connections required for experiencing physical emotions, or psychological problems caused for example by abnormal relationships during early development.

Pain is an experience felt in the mind. It is not simply there, but is learned during childhood as a response to various situations. The very small child does not cry because he is slapped but because of the anger expressed by his parents. Only subsequently does he learn to associate the slap with something unpleasant—pain. There are two types of learning or conditioning process that are relevant and analogies drawn from animal studies help us to understand human pain. When a dog sees food it forms profuse saliva in the mouth. If a bell is rung each time the food is offered, the dog will rapidly associate the bell with food and will even salivate when the bell rings alone without food being offered. This involuntary response is known as 'respondent conditioning'. On the other hand 'operant conditioning' occurs when an animal learns to press a bar because this is followed by the presentation of food. This is a voluntary process that has been learned.

Current concepts suggest that the outward expression of pain, such as wincing or crying is an example of operant conditioning. A child does something wrong, feels guilty, and experiences pain as a mechanism to expiate the guilt. It cries and is comforted by its mother. The comforting is a response that the child likes. It learns that crying means additional attention and care from its mother.

The theory is that pain and its outward expression such as complaining, groaning, wincing, etc., are maintained by compensations to the sufferer. This is not a deliberate decision but a subconscious reaction of the mind outside the individual's control. Compensation does not mean only monetary benefit but also other rewards such as sympathy and concern shown by relatives and friends, and being relieved of problems and responsibilities. In other words, there is a 'pay-off' which reinforces behaviour such as complaining about back pain and so encourages it to be repeated. The patient's spouse, family, friends, nurses, and doctors directly reinforce the pain by displaying sympathy, concern, and attention whenever pain is exprienced. The patient is given medicines and encouraged to rest while others assume his problems and responsibilities. Indirect reinforcement of pain arises by the patient avoiding those situations that may be thought likely to exacerbate the symptoms. Inactivity, inability to work and social isolation mean that he is unable to earn a living; this progressively results in self-perpetuating invalidism. The patient's spouse or relations may also reinforce dependency and invalidism. They encourage the patient to feel pain, perhaps because of an excessive need to care for an invalid, or even to alleviate their own psychological problems.

As pain behaviour has been maintained and encouraged by these reinforcers, treatment is aimed at reversing the pain-reward situation and altering the patient's behaviour. In some pain clinics, patients whose pain is believed to be caused in this way may be treated by a complex behaviour modification programme using operant conditioning. Normally, behaviour associated with pain such as complaining, wincing, groaning, crying, etc., would be treated with concerned attention, sympathy, and drugs which in practice only reinforce the symptoms in these people. In this programme, developed by a world-famous department in Seattle in the United States, the medical and nursing staff, with the prior full knowledge and consent of the patient and his relatives, ignore displays and if they develop either simply do not comment or discuss some other topic. The relatives and friends must also learn to ignore the illness behaviour and pain displays. Many of these patients are very inactive and behave as semi-invalids. A programme of gradual physical rehabilitation is introduced with specified physical activities each day, gradually increasing over several weeks. Successful performance of the required activities is encouraged and positively reinforced so that hopefully the patient gets back to something like a normal life.

The cynics suggest that this is how most physiotherapy treatment for the back works anyway. The optimism of most physiotherapists combined with encouragement to tackle progressively more difficult tasks and to return to normal physical activity may well be of far more value than the actual treatment itself.

Once it is decided that conventional medicine has nothing to offer, the patient and his relatives must avoid excessive consultations, investigations, prescriptions, and indulgent medical care. Finally, following successful treatment, positive reinforcement of well behaviour must continue to prevent the patient slipping back to his previous state. This may require supervision of retraining and return to work, and special counselling about individual problems. In particular, the patient must understand the basis of his or her problem. Cognitive behavioural treatments such as directed understanding and correcting patients' false beliefs about their symptoms and their causes are also useful.

Operant conditioning is particularly popular in the United States. It is not practised in exactly the same way in all clinics but the principles have been incorporated into various types of treatment programmes. The results are spectacularly successful in some cases but in others can be disappointing.

Personality and back pain

We all think we know what is meant by 'personality'. We recognize people as being of a particular type and think of them as cheerful, extrovert, difficult, and so on. However, these descriptions depend very much on whoever makes them and often there are completely contrasting views on the personality or an individual. The Prime Minister is honest, concerned, and sympathetic; or hard and an inveterate liar, according to one's politics. In an effort to provide more meaningful descriptions of personality, psychologists have developed a number of standard tests as objective measures of personality. These tests involve detailed questionnaries and often appear in very simplified or humorous forms in the newspapers as games or quizzes. These personality inventories have been used to study back pain patients to see if the chronic pain sufferer has a particular personality trait. Interpretation of the results of these questionnaires is not easy, especially as comparison between different ones show that they are not very reliable. However, interesting contrasts in the personalities of back suffereres arise between those whose symptoms are caused by a clear-cut and definite disorder such as a burst disc and those in whom physical examination and investigation have not found any abnormaility. The latter group show increased scores for hypochondriasis, which is the imagining of excessive illness, depression, and hysteria. A form of mental dissociation takes place as there are abnormal symptoms in the absence of any physical cause. such patients ae miserable, worried, and tense. They are convinced they suffer from a deep-seated illness despite evidence to the contrary. Their complaints may be the result of inner psychological conflicts and may be reinforced by a 'reward' as previously described. However, they will deny that their life problems and personalities affect the back pain in any way.

Can prolonged back pain cause these personality changes? After all it would not be too difficult to believe that persistent chronic disabling symptoms that fail to get better after repeated consulta-tions, investigations, medical treatment, and even operations, would have one miserable and depressed about the future. Psychologists and psychiatrists have addressed themselves to this chicken and egg problem of whether the pain causes personality changes or the abnormal personality causes the experience of pain. There is no easy answer but only clues from some recent studies. The psychological indices of patients severely and permanently paralysed because of poliomyelitis or other similar problems did not differ from those of normal people. In rheumatoid arthritis, psychological testing was normal in those with clear-cut disease but abnormal in those with symptoms but in whom the diagnosis was less certain. Those back sufferers who have an abnormal personality are less likely to respond well to medical or surgical treatment than those with normal personalities. These observations point to the personality having a fundamental role in the development and perpetuation of chronic illness. However, the question of which comes first may not be useful as the organic disease, the personality, and the pain interact with and build upon one another in complex and ill-understood fashions. What matters is understanding why the problem persists and what to do about it rather than how it started. There is scope for considerable further research.

Anxiety states and back pain

We all know what being anxious means—we feel tense and sweaty and the pulse rate increases. Normally anxiety is due to mental stress experienced for example before taking an examination or making a speech. However, an anxiety can develop as a psychological problem and produce back pain. In psychiatric terms, an abnormal anxiety state expresses itself in three main forms: as a sense of fear and tension without any obvious cause—this is known as free-floating anxiety; as unwarranted fear of a particular object or situation such as fear of enclosed spaces (claustrophobia); and as a physical symptom such as back pain.

Patients with an anxiety state develop abnormal contractions of the muscles of the trunk which are easily shown by electrical testing. These tense muscles are associated with aches and pains, particularly in the back as well as elsewhere. The muscle contractions are worse whenever anxiety increases and particularly in difficult and unpleasant situations. The patient feels the symptoms in these tense muscles so that the back pain is the result of the chronic anxiety state. Understanding the psychological basis of the problem indicates the treatment. The first step is to identify the physical, social and psychological stresses that may be responsible for the anxiety state.

Psychologists have developed various specialized methods for treating patients with anxiety states. Techniques for relaxation, distraction, and slow deep breathing exercises are often used. A diary is kept to record the pain and physical activities and a gradual increase in activity is planned. In biofeedback, the patient is given a degree of control over the symptoms by learning consciously to control an electrical signal which informs him about the amount of muscle tension. Hypnosis is an ill-understood mental state of heightened suggestability and sometimes provides better relief from tension than more straightforward treatment. Some patients receive training in relaxation techniques—that is, the achievement of a profound state of both mental and physical relaxation. These treatment methods may be combined with progressive desenstiza-tion to factors identified as responsible for the anxiety state. For example, fear of open spaces (agoraphobia) can be eliminated by a treatment programme introducing the patient gradually to more and more open environments, combined with relaxation procedures. The technique of operant conditioning has already been described.

Back pain and depression

We all feel depressed if a close friend or relative dies, we fail an examination, or some other disaster strikes. However, in psychiatric terms, depression refers to an excessively sad mood that may develop without any obvious cause or that is out of proportion to a relatively trivial or passing problem. Sometimes it may appear as 'masked' depression in which the depression is diguised as bodily symptoms and quite commonly as back pain and sciatica. On casual enquiry, the depression is not obvious and the patient may not be aware of it. However, there may be other features that make the diagnosis clear. In a study of back pain patients a poor response to conventional treatment correlated with a high incidence of depres-sion. Belief that depression causes pain rather than simply being a consequence of persistent back problems may suggest the use of anti-depressant drug therapy for such patients. Modern medicines are very successful in treating depression and helpful for back pain of this cause.

Back pain and sexual problems

Because of the direct and symbolic links of the back with the basic movements involved in sexual intercourse, it has been suggested that back disorders may be linked with sexual dysfunction. There is much speculation but little definite evidence about this. The most obvious reason for loss of interest or a decline in sexual performance is that intercourse produces severe back pain. This can simply be the result of mechanical stress on the spine rather than being due to any psychological causes. In a way, this is the easiest problem to deal with as sympathetic understanding by the partner combined with simple practical advice may be all that is required. A firm bed, a board under the mattress, a pillow in the small of the back or a reversal of positions can help enormously. Some back sufferers take pain-relieving tablets about half an hour in advance.

Depression and chronic anxiety states can cause loss of libido and failure to achieve an erection. In its turn, this gives rise to further conflict and anxiety, which perpetuates the problem. Often such patients will not discuss their difficulties and so the problem becomes magnified, deep-rooted, and intractable. Appropriate treatment by medical or psychological means can help enormously.

Finally, a pre-existing sexual problem may provide a deliberate or subconscious motive for the complaint of back pain. The impotent husband who injures his back may discover that his pain provides an acceptable excuse for avoiding sex in the same way that the proverbial headache exempts the wife from the unwelcome attentions of her partner.

Management of the psychological aspects of back pain

It is clear that there is a complex interplay between the physical responses to problems in the back and the human mind. A full medical assessment requires the doctor to consider the psychological and social aspects of the problem and if necessary to institute appropriate treatment. This may be a combination of physical treatment with drugs to lessen anxiety and control depression. Assessment of the patient's personality, past and present, and of any stressful events can suggest psychological therapy such as behaviour modification techniques and exploration and adjustment of the patient's social relationships with his family, friends, and work. The relationship between back pain and the mind is complex and must always be considered carefully by those caring for back pain sufferers.

Glossary

acupuncture: a system originally developed in China for relieving pain by insertion of needles into the skin.

ankylosing spondylitis: a disorder most common in young men, producing inflammation in the joints of the spine and occasionally elsewhere, together with back pain. It may lead to progressive stiffness and deformity.

annulus fibrosus: the fibrous outer layer of the intervertebral dis.

arachnoiditis: a condition of scarring of the nerve roots which may be severely damaged.

chiropractic: a system for manipulation of the spine.

enthesis: the junction of tendon and bone.

epidural injection: an injection into the vertebral canal. Local anaesthetic and cortisone are used in this way to relieve the symptoms of back pain.

HLA B27: the white cell type that predisposes to the development of ankylosing spondylitis.

intervertebral disc: the flat cushion which lies between the bodies of the vertebrae.

ischial tuberosities: the twin bones within the buttocks which carry the weight of the body when sitting.

Kinetic handling techniques: manual methods of lifting and carrying heavy objects which minimize the risk of injury to the back.

kyphosis: an unnatural forward angulation of the spine.

lumbago: an acute attack of pain in the lumbar region.

lumbar lordosis: the backwards curvature of the lower back or lumber region.

manipulation: treatment of back pain by manual pressure.

nucleus pulposus: the gelatinous (jelly-like) centre of the intervertebral disc.

osteopathy: a form of manipulation of the back which is used by certain medical and non medical practitioners.

osteomalacia: weakness of the bones because of calcium deficiency. It may be due to poor diet, lack of sunlight, or failure to absorb nutrients and vitamins properly from the bowel.

osteoporosis: weakness of the bones due to a deficient fibrous framework. It may occur in older people, particularly women, as a result of lack of sex hormones, certain diseases, and after taking certain drugs.

prolapsed intervertebral disc: a burst of the disc backwards and usually to one side or the other, producing damage to nerve roots and the symptoms of pain in the back and the lower limb.

sacro-iliac joints: the joints between the sacrum or tailbone and the pelvis.

sciatica: pain felt in the back of the thigh and in the leg due to damage of the nerve roots by a burst intervertebral disc.

scoliosis: a twisting of the spine which sometimes develops in children or may develop in response to damage inside the back.

slipped disc: a misnomer for a prolapsed intervertebral disc.

spinal stenosis: narrowing of the vertebral canal so that the nerve roots are at greater risk of damage.

spondylosis: wear and tear damage of the spine.

trancutaneous nerve stimulation: an electrical method of stimulating the back which may reduce the sensation of pain in a similar fashion to acupuncture.

trigger points: localized areas of extreme tenderness in the back.

vertebra: one of the elements making up the spinal column.

Organizations for back pain patients

Below are listed some of the national and international societies and organizations which are concerned with back pain. These bodies will be pleased to offer advice, information, and assistance. However, they are only able to deal with enquiries in general terms. For individual problems patients should refer to their own family doctor and the specialist and paramedical services at his disposal.

Arthritis and Rheumatism Council
Copeman House, St Mary's Court, St. Mary's Gate, Chesterfield, Derbyshire S41 7TO

Arthritis Care
6 Grosvenor Crescent, London SW1X 7ER

National Back Pain Association
31–33 Park Road, Teddington, Middx., TW11 0AB

National Ankylosing Spondylitis Society
6 Grosvenor Crescent, London SW1X 7ER

National Osteoporosis Society
Barton Meade House, PO Box 10, Haydon, Radstock, Nr Bath, BA3 3YB

Spinal Injuries Association
76 St James' Lane, London N10 3DF

European League Against Rheumatism
Witikonstrasse 68, CH–8032, Zurich, Switzerland

International League Against Rheumatism
B. P. 145, CH–4011 Basle, Switzerland

Arthritis Foundation
1314 Spring St. NW, Atlanta, Georgia 30309, USA

Australian Arthritis Foundation
3rd Floor, Wingello House, Sydney, NSW 2000, Australia

The Arthritis Society
Suite 401, 250 Bloor St. E., Toronto, Ontario, Canada M4W 3P2

The Arthritis Foundation of New Zealand
PO Box 10–020, 150 Featherston Street, Wellington, New Zealand

South African Arthritis Foundation
709 Tulbagh Centre, Hans Strydom Avenue, Foreshore, Cape Town 8001,
South Africa

Index